T0209657

Farewell
to my father

Paul Vrolijk

WESTBOW
PRESS®
A DIVISION OF THOMAS NELSON
& ZONDERVAN

WestBow Press books may be ordered through booksellers or by contacting:

WestBow Press
A Division of Thomas Nelson & Zondervan
1663 Liberty Drive
Bloomington, IN 47403
www.westbowpress.com
844-714-3454

ISBN: 979-8-3850-0112-5 (sc)
ISBN: 979-8-3850-0113-2 (hc)
ISBN: 979-8-3850-0114-9 (e)

Library of Congress Control Number: 2023911191

Print information available on the last page.

WestBow Press rev. date: 09/14/2023

Nothing can separate us from the love of God.

—Based on Romans 8:38–39

In loving memory of my father

Gerrit Dirk Vrolijk
Dick

Scheveningen, 11 July 1937

Sassenheim, 12 October 2022

This book is dedicated to all who loved and cared for my father. You will find yourselves on the following pages. I write this in tremendous gratitude to you!

Contents

Introduction

A Blessed Hello and Farewell

WELCOME TO A FAREWELL. I HOPE YOU WILL JOIN ME FOR A BRIEF JOURNEY that took only a few months but that lovingly brought a life together and to an end—the life of my father. I write this in thankful memory of him. It all happened fairly quickly. It took a mere three months from the moment my father was admitted to the hospital, and then hospice, his death, his funeral, and the sale of the house. When I started writing this, I had no idea whether this would be a few pages or a book. It did not matter. I intended to stop when the flow of loving memory in ink stopped. The loving flow of memories in my heart will never cease.

The idea to write came days after my father had died and was buried. My relationship with my father has been a really good one. I realize how blessed I am. I do not think my father understood everything about me, but that did not matter. He questioned some of my choices, but there was never any regret. He always supported me and always wanted the best for me. We loved one another. We can fully love without fully understanding. Love surpasses understanding, a bit like peace.

Like all of us, my father had some interesting quirks. When they appear on these pages, they are lovingly remembered. In my family, we can make fun of one another, but always in love. It helps not to take oneself too seriously.

I also want to salute my father's care in preparing various things for when he would not be there anymore. These were mostly very practical, administrative things. Some of these preparations he started to plan many years ago (e.g., saving for his grandchildren), and some took place in the closing days of his life. There has been much here to encourage me in preparing for my own death. When that day comes, I hope I will be as prepared as my father was. I hope this will inspire and encourage you to think about your own death. That may strike you as odd, but pondering our deaths can be great fuel for living well—a bit of resurrection power flowing back into this side of life.

Whatever the best efforts of my father, a good death is a gift from God. I want to thank our Heavenly Father, who brought everything together in the closing weeks of my father's life. The faith strand in this story is an important one—probably the most important one in lovingly stitching the different, seemingly boring, pieces of our lives together. For my father, with some of his struggles in faith and loss, God graciously worked for the good in all things. I can really say that, even from a position of limited understanding. I would call that invisible divine touch miraculous. It wove the glorious into the mundane, the sacred tapestry of life. If you are reading this and your relationship with your earthly father has been difficult, compromised, or nonexistent, I hope that what stands out from these pages is that you have a Heavenly Father who is watching over you and who lovingly cares for you. If you doubt the possibility of that, just read the story of what took place and allow what is hidden on these pages to seep into your mind and heart.

Writing has given me much joy. It has allowed me to remember my father again, and it has also allowed me to ponder the deeper lessons of his departure. I hope this book will bring encouragement, comfort, joy and inspiration to you who will be reading this. Maybe there are some ideas on how to prepare for your own departure, or maybe a gentle reminder to discuss certain things with your father or mother before that moment comes. Take and receive what is useful for you.

I feel the need to add some disclaimers here. For those who seek brilliant theology, I need to disappoint you. What I have penned is very down-to-earth, simple stuff. I do not apologize. For me theology needs to be practical anyway. It needs to help us to keep it all together in order to help make sense of life and God, without losing hope, life, beauty, or mystery. Our thinking, writing, and speaking about God should never be a mere vanity project. This certainly isn't. Names of people and places have been mostly omitted to make it easier for you to engage with the story.

That's my hope. For those who cannot live with such ambiguity, some place names have been provided at the end of this book.

May the Lord bless you and keep you! You are loved and cared for. The elements of your life *are* being lovingly stitched together. I hope and pray that in your journey you may perceive how all things hang together, and that you may see glimpses of the One at work through it all.

Joyfully in Him,
Paul

Before You Read On

It might be handy for you to know a little bit about my family. My father was born in 1937, and my mother in 1940. They both lived through World War II as children in the occupied Netherlands. They grew up in the same village and married in 1962. In 1964, I was born; and in 1968, my sister joined the crowd. In 1970, we moved to the village and the house where my father would live for the next fifty-two years. I married in 1992. My mother died in 1993. My sister married in 2000. We are both still married and have children, all of them teenagers or young adults. My father died in October 2022.

Home

Coffee

I WALK UP THE DRIVEWAY. MY CAR IS PARKED AROUND THE CORNER. There is no sign of life. My father is probably busy in the kitchen preparing coffee—coffee which had become weaker over the years, though Janine and I did not want to mention that to him. We had tried various schemes to improve this aspect of our get-togethers. "We'll make the coffee when we arrive! Don't worry." But my father had firmly resisted and insisted he keep doing it himself. My father was like that, which we had come to accept, and at times even love. It certainly was good material for sibling debriefings. I walked past the kitchen window, and there he was, bent over, preparing the coffee we were about to share. White-haired and smaller, he was peering into the coffee filter. My father had grown old. He was eighty-five now, still living in the house we had moved into fifty-two years ago. My mom had passed away nearly thirty years ago. Not much had changed in the house since, and that was absolutely fine. Actually, everything *needed* to stay the same. A few months prior, my sister had taken it upon herself to remove all the pans from the kitchen. After all, my father never cooked. Was it not better if handy drawer space was used for foodstuffs and items he used regularly? All within easy reach? It was a perfect plan—and doomed to fail. She clearly had underestimated our father's indestructible resolve. When everybody had left for the day, my father, with his poor legs, went up and down the narrow and steep cellar stairs to retrieve the misplaced pans and restore them to their mom-ordained places in the cupboards—everything exactly where it should be. "Change? Over my dead body, thank you very much." We smiled afterward and dutifully reprimanded him for taking such unnecessary risks. Will I become like him? What is the percentage of mom in me in this particular genetic area?

I turned right through the garden door, and right again, and came to the back door, which was unlocked. This was not always the case. The back door key was safely kept in his top drawer of his desk, below his comb. Security first, convenience much later. I opened the door and the fly door and stepped into the kitchen. There he was, my elderly father, leaning against the work surface, careful to keep his balance. His walking and standing had slowly deteriorated over the years, an open wound in his left leg being the culprit—a wound that defied healing despite much effort by doctors and carers. His quality of life was slowly seeping away. It was difficult to watch. It was also difficult to be carelessly cheerful while he was in so much pain. We spoke regularly on the phone, and conversations always started with talk of "the leg." I completely understood. Eventually the conversation would drift to gratitude. Gratitude mostly shone through, eventually. It needed to be dug up and brushed off, but it was always there. My father slowly made his way to me, and I to him. We embraced in a warm, loving hug that had become bonier over the years. I smelled my father. That unique, precious smell offered a feast of recognition.

I looked into his tired eyes. He looked at me, asking me how the journey was and where I had parked. ("Always the same place, Dad.") How was Janine? How were the kids? He was in pain. "I am not sure how much longer I can carry on like this." His walking had further deteriorated over the last few months. He gave me an update on the latest. The ongoing battle by medics and carers to make the best of a difficult situation was drawing to a close. His leg had been a problem for many years as a result of poor circulation—something he had in common with his mother. I remember that when she would bump her leg against a table, the wound would take months to close and properly heal, only to be opened again at the next bump. This problem was with her for many years. My father had claimed his genetic inheritance. His wounds, however, had become more problematic. They had become infected on several occasions. All sorts of things had been tried, including careful cleaning and various antibiotics. Nothing had really resolved the problem. My father's lifelong sedentary lifestyle probably did not help. He had engaged in office work for life, but that had stopped twenty years prior. He had done a little bit of cycling back then; a bit of walking, but not that much; and no physical exercise besides some shopping and little tasks in the house. A simple home trainer we had given him a few years before was not used that much. Anyway, all of that was too late now, it seemed. However, he certainly was not overweight. My father had the opposite problem. He was quite thin and not really eating that well. Fortunately, some warm meals were prepared for him throughout the weeks. People sometimes stayed to make sure he really ate it and did not store it for days to come. All these habits were now coming together in a slowly accelerating downward turn.

Gratitude

Fortunately my father had a network of people looking after him, from doctors and carers who looked after the wound to friends and neighbors who, over the years, had divided the day-to-day shopping and practical help around the house. My sister and her family lived an hour-and-a-half drive away. For the last seven years, my family and I had lived nearly three hours away. Before then we had lived even farther away abroad. My father never complained. He was proud of his children, and then grandchildren, and their diverse developments and achievements. We spoke regularly on the phone. Several years ago, that had been once a week. Recently it had become more frequent.

He allowed me to pour the coffee. This was new. He leaned on the work surface to open the fridge to get some milk. I could have done that too. He allowed me to carry the tray and cups—something I had been allowed to do for the last year or so. Progressively he had been able to do less. He slowly made his way to the living room with his walker and let himself fall onto the sofa. I took a place on the adjacent one. We drank our coffee. We talked some more about the leg, his carers, the care of the neighbors, and the meals that were provided over the last few days. As lament petered out, gratitude emerged. It almost always did. My father was grateful. Gratitude was at the center of his being.

Gratitude is so important. Gratitude is such a gift. When you are grateful, you are doubly blessed. How much more precious do we experience life and its small blessings when we have gratitude. "Small blessings," is not quite an accurate phrase. Every blessing is a blessing, and a blessing is never less than great. Appreciating the so-called small things in life is a blessing. Normality infused with hidden delight is precious.

We talked some more. We covered administrative duties—an important topic for my dad. My sister was taking more care of this. It had evolved naturally and was a good solution. We spoke of gratitude again. We then turned to faith, the leg, Janine, kids, shopping, eating, and administration, and then we returned to faith. We were working our usual list. It was wonderfully familiar.

Faith had been difficult at times for my father. It was less controllable than shopping and administration, but so much more important. There were two topics that recurred in some form or another over the years: "Why did Jeanne have to die so young?" and "What about the resurrection?" I knew these questions came not come from theological curiosity, but from sadness and loss. My father greatly missed my mom. We both knew there was no satisfactory answer to this first question. Whatever direction that particular conversation took, eventually we would arrive again at gratitude—for his marriage, his children, and his grandchildren, as well as for the contact we had and for the way we were blessed in so many ways. But loss was real and lingering. The question regarding the resurrection and what happened after death was trickier. The reason for that was the world in which my father lived, so full of doubt and denial, even in church. He doubted God and his resurrection life and power. How blessed we are to just live with the mysterious and to count on the miraculous. How wonderful it is to just receive and accept, having a deep knowing that transcends mere explanations and knowing we are known from eternity to eternity. Knowing the One is more important than knowing all the answers. We trust. That is faith first and foremost—when you *know* you know. It is not a figment of one's imagination.

Struggle

I mentioned two issues in the previous section: the loss of mom, and Dad's occasional doubt. Thinking back, I am surprised there was not a third—suffering. His suffering. Aside from a very occasional outburst (stemming from a volatile temper he had when he was younger, about which I will shortly relate a funny story), he carried his current suffering patiently. The biblical word would be "longsuffering." He was resigned to the inevitability of it all.

My father's father could make everything. What his eyes saw, his hands could make. My father did not inherit that gifting. TTDIY (try to do it yourself) was something my father did not relish. Actually it always became quite a big thing—something that would take an evening or a morning, though skilled people could do it in fifteen minutes, or so they would like to believe. My grandfather had made quite a number of things in the house that were still standing fifty years later. I can still see him fixing things in the heat of summer. My paternal grandparents would come over for a few days at a time. My grandfather always loved to have a little list of projects to work on, and afterward he would have a nice, cool beer in the garden. I loved my grandparents. They were all very different, but I am so glad to have known them all and to have enjoyed all of them in their own ways, through sleepovers and other activities.

One of the things my grandfather had made for the bedrooms upstairs were roll-on screens to keep out the bugs. Now, if you unhooked those screens at the bottom and let them shoot up—Oops!—the wooden edge would come flying off. My father would then have to repair this with glue and patience. One fine Saturday morning, my sister (four years younger) and I were teasing each other as siblings do. I say "each other," but being the older one (nine at the time, I believe), I probably should take full responsibility for this episode. Anyway, my father—probably leaning over the dreaded project upstairs, cursing his fate of being "the man in the house," and hating the fact that we had again ignored his parental advice to let go of the screen gently—asked us to stop fooling around. We did not listen (read: *I* did not listen). We happily carried on with the annoying banter downstairs till we heard him explode. My fight-or-flight reflexes were impeccably sharpened by eons of evolution. This time my response was flight, of course! My father was racing through the bedroom and entering the landing upstairs. I was groping the front door, trying desperately to open it. He came racing down the stairs. I kept wriggling the key to open the door. My father, and impending death, were near; and oh, blessed release, the door opened! I raced out of the front garden just beyond his grasp. On my house slippers, I scrambled over the pavement to safety around the corner, and then to the left. A hymn of praise was rising in my heart, or at least a brief prayer of thanks. Opposite our house, the butcher shop was filled with Saturday-morning clients looking with surprise in our direction. What on earth was going on? I couldn't care. I was safe. I ran around the corner and stayed away at a safe distance.

I knew from experience that my father could be very angry, but he could never stay angry for very long. Normally a bit of time, an apology and smile, and a funny remark would clear the air. I took a bit longer this day, just to be sure. I returned to the house eventually and made my way upstairs, feeling contrite. I found him bent over the dreaded gluing project, peering over the handiwork. I apologized and tried a funny remark. He grumbled. I knew we were good. Another precious family memory was born. God is good, all the time.

Prayer

Back to suffering in the current age. Bandages lay next to me in a small pile on the sofa. They were washed earlier that week. He would fold them (for whatever reason)—a project that would take him substantial time. Behind the sofa was his walker and a box with more medical items in it. His suffering was evident all around. However, he did not complain much. The final item on our list was drawing near. My father made the point that he prayed daily and that he always prayed for us. He never lost his faith, but he had his doubts, his questions, and sometimes a complaint. I never felt concern. God could handle it. We prayed. Sometimes I offered, and sometimes he asked, but our recent visits had always concluded with prayer. We held my father in prayer, but it was even better to pray together. It was nothing elaborate—just simple trust. Again that word. "Natural" would be better. I hope you know what I mean.

I offered to wash the cups and clear up. My father accepted. I washed the cups and put everything into its proper place. We embraced. I kissed him. He wished me well for the journey. I gathered my stuff and put on my coat. Yes, I would call when I had arrived. We loved one another. I went out as I had come and walked around the house. I waved when I was in front. I thought I saw him wave back. How long would he be able to carry on like this?

Hospital

Open Skies

IT WAS A BEAUTIFUL SUNNY AUTUMN DAY, NOT A CLOUD IN THE SKY. OPEN pasture spread around me, holding me up as I sped along on a narrow, moist dark gray strip in a vast green plane. Clouds of starlings were doing their synchronicity thing. The rush hour had not been too bad. I was making good time, but I needed to take a break. After a while, relief came into sight. As I hastily closed my car door, the dampness of the grass grounded me in earthy familiarity. I smelled the fresh morning air. I returned to the car and poured a small cup of strong coffee from my thermos. I could stay here longer, but I need to drive on. I longed to see my father. Thoughts of worry and the sad realization that human life is finite pervaded my mind. The open skies were so immense. So wide. Natural beauty was upholding me. Glory was totally embracing the contained mortal concerns in the smallness of my car.

Having driven for another hour, I found a parking place with a nice picnic bench behind a service station. The world was racing by on one side, and I was experiencing the glories of pasture and trees on another. I parked in between the two. I stepped out of the car and stretched my legs, inhaling the still, cool autumn air and enjoying the mild sun on my face. The picnic bench was waiting for me. Bliss. I consumed a lovingly prepared sandwich and went back to the thermos of coffee again. Here I experienced fifteen minutes of rest and space. I felt blessed. Life was good. I was thankful.

My father was in the hospital—or, better stated, back in the hospital. A few days ago, he had been admitted but had quickly released himself.

My sister and I had shaken our heads. That evening, things had not gone well. In a dark and difficult night, my father realized he had acted too rashly. He was back in the emergency room in the morning. The wound on his leg had become worse over the last few months. Despite a great support network of carers, neighbors, and friends, he was no longer able to look after himself. That was a hard fact to swallow. My father, normally clean shaven and neatly dressed, was now not able to do what he had done for over eighty years—wash and dress himself. Discussions had taken place with the doctors in the hospital as to what could be done. Another discussion would take place this afternoon. What would be next?

Hospital

I arrived at the regional hospital around midday, as planned. This was a new hospital, in a new location. Several decades ago, my mother had worked in the hospital that had preceded this one, much closer to home—a cycle ride away. On a few nights each week, she took the evening shift at the intensive care unit, noticing increased traffic when football was on television. This new hospital was vast. At least that's how it seemed to me. All those who were entering seemed to know where they were going. I felt like a provincial in the city, but then reversed. Having found the parking exit, I joined the stream of mostly elderly visitors. They had the time to do the necessary.

After some initial searching (my goodness, this is a big place), I found the ward where my father lay, a few floors up. All these wards looked the same. I scanned the doors for numbers and clues. There he was, in a room with a large bed for himself. The usual trappings of hospitalization lay dotted around. My father seemed a lot smaller than when I had left him a few weeks prior. He was wearing his familiar light blue pajamas. He was glad to see me. He looked unshaven, uncombed, and ashen, but he was totally my lovely father. We greeted one another with a bony hug, cheek to cheek. Yes, he was quite unshaven. We shared a kiss. I asked him how he was. He was so-so. No reason to complain. He had been better. He should not have returned home earlier that week. This sounded like a confession to me. It had been unwise and dangerous. He could see that now. I nodded, silently granting absolution. We smiled. They were looking after him well. Some things would happen that afternoon, but he was not completely certain what.

Our opening chatter was disrupted by a cheerful nurse. "I have come to take Mr. Vrolijk away." She did not have all the details but said all would be well. They would try something to ease his pain from the knee down. That sounded like an excellent plan. I was not in a rush. I had assumed my outing would take the whole day.

A few minutes after my father had been wheeled out, a lady came in to serve his warm meal—a sturdy brunette, not in her best mood. I assumed she had better moods, surely. I mentioned she had just missed my father. "Well … I cannot do much about that." She firmly placed the tray down on the side table and left. She appeared a bit out of place. Or was she the foil against whom the others could shine brighter? Every person so far had shown such care and forbearance. I assumed it was probably just a bad day for her.

It was time for me to read, think, reminisce, and be bored. I went downstairs to get a coffee and sit in the spacious welcome area. I was reading a bit, but mostly watching people—especially people entering the restrooms. It was so interesting to observe the search, the sometimes anxious gazes, and then relief. The seekers were old and young, male and female, smooth and staggering, pretty and less so, all of them united by a common need. I like to be bored. It is a welcome contrast to being 'on' and busy, which has been the default for most of my life. After an hour, I returned upstairs, thinking he would surely be back soon.

My father stayed away for two and a half hours. He finally returned to the room and was famished. A kind nurse offered to microwave his meal. I watched him empty his plate at speed. It was a clean sweep. Having finished his food, he was happy to have some more. Some coffee and *ontbijtkoek* with butter? Yes, he would love to try some of the chocolate I brought as well. It was great to see him with such an appetite.

Shortly after he had finished his meal, a doctor appeared. He introduced himself. My sister and I had spoken with him over the phone a few days before. His specialty was vascular surgery. A female doctor colleague joined us as well. Her specialty was palliative care. My sister was dialed in as well. Both doctors were so humane, friendly, and patient. The first doctor repeated the highlights of our earlier conversation. Because the various treatments over the last years had not been able to deal with the infection in my father's leg structurally, and because of his deteriorating situation, the only real possibility left to stop the infection was amputation above the knee. I looked at my father. He sat in silence, propped against his pillows. We had discussed this option in various conversations over the previous few weeks, and my father was not keen. I could understand. A younger version of my father would probably have gone for it eventually, but after much deliberation. Now this seemed a bridge too far. He would need several months of revalidation. Normally people on one leg manage to be quite mobile by hopping on one leg for short distances and using a wheelchair for longer ones. The reality was that hopping on one leg did not seem to be a practical solution for my father at this stage. To survive for a number of years being fairly immobile was not attractive for him.

The doctor concluded the first bit of his advice by listing the usual disclaimers regarding operational success and risk, and then patiently observed my father to see how the message had landed. I admired the blend of professionalism, patience, and kindness. My father remained silent. The doctor continued by explaining the alternative. Because all antibiotics had failed and my father's circulation was poor, amputation really was the only method to slow the deadly and certain decline. If my father would decide not to allow the amputation, he would not be treated any longer (in order to try to heal him), and the palliative care phase would commence. The other doctor took over. She was similarly professional, patient, and kind. Brother and sister I wondered. She started by explaining the procedure that had taken place earlier in the afternoon. A procedure had been undertaken to block the pain in my father's leg from the knee downward on a more permanent basis. It was an experiment—her idea. If it worked, they would do it again the next day, so that my father would be pain-free for several weeks, maybe even for a few months. That sounded wonderful. We thanked her for proposing and arranging it.

My father queried regarding various options, including care homes and hospice. The doctor assured my father that he would receive the best care in the hospice. Their mission and ethos were completely geared toward that. A hospice nearby my sister was proposed so she could visit my father regularly; this would be more challenging for her if he remained where he was now. A life expectancy of three months was mentioned. This was quickly followed by the possibility that if his situation stabilized and his life expectancy appeared to lengthen, he could be placed in a care home. The second doctor finished her explanation and with equal compassion watched how her explanation had been received.

My father looked into the distance and pondered. He then slowly returned to the present and carefully started to argue for a middle way—no amputation, but still living on for five years. Both doctors smiled patiently, but not unkindly. It was explained that this particular via media sadly did not exist. My father's gaze showed one of acceptance.

Open Skies Once More

The doctors left. The telephone conversation with my sister ended. My father had some thinking to do. I looked outside. The same massive blue sky that had embraced me this morning on my way was holding us now. The silent glory was so assuring. I lowered my sight. Between the hospital wing where my father was and some lower buildings a bit further down, a beautiful acacia basked in the sunshine, the leaves a light yellow-green, emitting a translucent glow. My father lived on Acacia Lane. God had provided a bit of home away from home. Still home, but different. He mentioned that he clearly would not be returning to his house. Again there was that acceptance I had witnessed during my conversation with the doctors. I stood in awe. My father would not be returning to the house where he had lived for fifty-two years—the house that had been so precious to him. I had expected that this would be the real difficult thing, but it was not. It was released. Just like that. Or had he been doing some thinking already? My father was very realistic about what would follow over the coming weeks, possibly months. We did some thinking aloud. The doctors clearly made an impression. We again discussed the various options with their pros and cons. He leaned toward the hospice option, where they really were geared toward taking care of him in his last weeks or months. He would think some more. We left it at that.

A Funeral Commissioned

My father turned to me. "Can you contact my vicar? Ask her to lead my service when the moment comes. Can you preach? Please choose readings that give hope." I accepted the mission. His vicar had been attentive, especially over the last few months. She had visited him here in hospital. Being asked by my father to preach now felt the most normal thing in the world. I realized this might not be easy on the day, but that did not matter. I was pleased at how normal this request now sounded. My becoming a vicar has a bit of a history to it. Let me bore you with a brief summary of events.

At a young age (six, probably), having just moved to the village, I had pondered my future career options. My thoughts at the time were that I wanted to be a doctor during the week and the vicar on Sunday—a choice more informed by an awareness of which figures were considered important in the village than a clear understanding of what both these callings entailed. I smiled at my silly thoughts. I am thankful for having grown up in a Christian family. I was baptized as a baby. We went to church since as far back as I can remember. In the village, we went to church on Sunday mornings, and sometimes even for a second time in the evening. We said grace before and after meals. We read the Bible after dinner. Mostly this went by uneventfully, although I remember one occasion when we ventured into Revelation and read the passage on the woman and the dragon. It left us all confused, but no attempt was made to find an explanation. This was well before we could whip out our smartphones and consult Google. We were also encouraged to pray before we went to bed. All this was well understood. It did not need to be discussed or explained. This is how it was. Looking back, it might have been a bit obligatory and mechanical. However, I am grateful for these early faith (or, better, church) experiences, as they gave me a certain direction.

In my teenage years, I became more resistant. One of the things I found strange was that our vicar would always pray for the "nice" professionals, such as doctors and nurses, but never for people in industry or in business, which I perceived to be my future places of work. A signal was sent that those occupations were considered less Christian than others. At least that is how I heard it. When I shared with my vicar that I was thinking about studying applied physics, he mumbled that people often lose their faith when they go to university. This was another signal that I was heading into unsanctioned territory.

On my eighteenth birthday, I declared to my parents that now that I was eighteen, I would never go to church again. During my university years, however, I was not that consistent in staying away. When I visited my parents, I would join them at church on a Sunday, but personal prayer and Bible reading did not happen. God, however, was good and faithful, and would draw me back over time. My parents had responded somewhat sadly, but we did not discuss it at great length, maybe because my decision so fitted with the overall trends at the time. Kids my age were almost expected to drop away. I grew up in a church in which dropping away was the norm. In all my childhood years, I never witnessed anyone coming to faith. Fortunately, that would change.

Twenty-four years ago, my faith came alive. It started through warm and solid preaching in a Dutch Reformed church in the city where I studied, but our awakening came more fully in Singapore, in an Anglican church through an Alpha course. The Holy Spirit day, on May 23, 1998, was the turning point in my life. Briefly after that, I felt a call into ordained ministry. These few sentences do no justice to the radical shift in my life, but that is not the subject of my writing here. My mother was not alive anymore, but I regularly discussed my plans with my father. For two and a half years, every Sunday, my father would ask, "Are you really sure, Paul?" I think my vocation was being tested! During the first few years of my new direction, my father was not sure I had opted for the right thing. Would my family survive? Would Janine and I be able to provide for our children? All these concerns were gradually dealt with.

Initially my father had felt loss for me having given up an international career and a job that paid well, and all the so-called prestige that came with that. Gradually he had come to accept my so-called late calling. I certainly understood his initial shock and hesitation when I informed him about my calling into full-time ministry. He had been present for my ordination and my installation into my current post, and he had enjoyed the exciting post that was. Later, when I became archdeacon, I was able to visit him fairly regularly on my way to or from churches I was visiting. He had found new pride in my ecclesiastical endeavors, although I do not think that was always the appropriate sentiment. It did not matter; I knew it came from love. He now asked me to preach at his funeral, a journey of acceptance completed.

He also asked me to maintain a good relationship with my sister. It is difficult to dictate good relationships, but I understood what he meant. He had asked this in the past. It clearly was something that was weighing on his mind. I assured him that this was what we all wanted. Our growing up had been harmonious. In primary and secondary school, my sister had grown annoyed with the question "Are you Paul's sister?" So when she went to study law in a different place from where I was studying applied physics, she was delighted to be able to make a mark for herself. Interestingly, it was through my sister that I met my wife, but that is another story. Growing up we had always remained in regular touch, but the spiritual awakening of me and my wife had been puzzling to her, and I think she continued to find it difficult to ask about my life and work, although that had become a bit easier over the years as well. Anyway, keeping a good relationship was something we all wanted. It was also very important to my father.

"Shall we read something and then pray?" I asked. I proposed to read the end of Romans 8. My father nodded. I knew that the glorious end of Romans 8 had been the wedding text for my parents. I was drawn to a verse a bit earlier in that chapter, verse 18, where it says, "For I consider that the sufferings of this present time are not worth comparing with the glory that is to be revealed to us." I read it slowly and looked up to see how those words had landed.

My father nodded, his hands folded in silent acceptance. "Yes, that's how it is …"

My father had journeyed in all sorts of ways. This was significant: the almost businesslike acceptance by him, trusted assurance of "glory to be revealed", eternal glory enfolding and surpassing temporary suffering, a vast blue expanse enfolding a new hospital building full of temporary suffering of various kinds. This hospital room held, like my car, the cumulative suffering still small in comparison to the enfolding glory. How wonderful it was to see that reality. What fuel for our hope. That would be one text for his funeral, surely.

I continued to slowly read the rich, dense text of glory. We were on holy ground.

For the creation waits with eager longing for the revealing of the sons of God. For the creation was subjected to futility, not willingly, but because of him who subjected it, in hope that the creation itself will be set free from its bondage to corruption and obtain the freedom of the glory of the children of God. For we know that the whole creation has been groaning together in the pains of childbirth until now. And not only the creation, but we ourselves, who have the firstfruits of the Spirit, groan inwardly as we wait eagerly for adoption as sons, the redemption of our bodies.

Bondage, corruption, groaning. What amazing depth and significance in those words received in my father's present suffering on this glorious afternoon, in the process of taking a momentous decision. He might well have made the decision already and was in the process of moving toward a new landmark and new destiny, which had been there all the time but which was now more clearly acknowledged. He was preparing himself. He was already more ready than I had ever expected him to be.

Then we came to a beautiful pinnacle of hope, a midway resting point on our way to the summit of glory and assurance: "For in this hope we were saved. Now hope that is seen is not hope. For who hopes for what he sees? But if we hope for what we do not see, we wait for it with patience." Hope! The longing of my father was echoed so clearly in this familiar passage we were reading through. My father was reminded through these ancient and inspired words, so full of life, truth, and hope, of what he asked and longed for—hope that will not disappoint. Hope is something we can wait for with patience, in complete trust, and, yes, in the midst of suffering. This life was coming to a close.

Then came some wonderful verses on the work of the Holy Spirit, who was so at work in our present situation in this holy moment: "Likewise the Spirit helps us in our weakness." Again I was looking at my father in all his terminal human weakness, who was needing and receiving all the help he could hope for. "For we do not know what to pray for as we ought," St. Paul continues, "but the Spirit himself intercedes for us with groanings too deep for words. And he who searches hearts knows what is the mind of the Spirit, because the Spirit intercedes for the saints according to the will of God." What an assurance when we feel our prayers are as utterly weak and feeble as our decaying bodies. Looking back, I could see that so many of our prayers were pedestrian when we started, till a holy glow ascended and filled our simple utterances with holy longing and grounded faith. Yes, the Lord is here; his Spirit is with us! And the solid assurance of that verse is so comforting and strengthening the moment we start to take it on board in all its fullness: "And we know that for those who love God all things work together for good for those who are called according to his purpose." We both sensed and knew the deep truth of that statement in our current circumstances. My father knew that he was loved by God, that he was held, that he was blessed, and that God would see him through this last difficult bit. This chapter mentions "groaning," yes, but also "the redemption of our bodies."

Then there was another deeply dense passage about God knowing us before we came into being, "us" referring to the ones he called, the ones who were made right with him to be "glorified" when that moment would come. This is a reference to the bit when we die and will be with him forever. This is our resurrection hope—our glorious future, given us through Jesus Christ. We did not dwell on that. It was too much to ponder for what my father needed now. We moved to his wedding text, which starts in verse 31:

> What then shall we say to these things? If God is for us, who can be against us? He who did not spare his own Son but gave him up for us all, how will he not also with him graciously give us all things? Who shall bring any charge against God's elect? It is God who justifies. Who is to condemn? Christ Jesus is the one who died—more than that, who was raised—who is at the right hand of God, who indeed is interceding for us. Who shall separate us from the love of Christ? Shall tribulation, or distress, or persecution, or famine, or nakedness, or danger, or sword? As it is written,
>
> "For your sake we are being killed all the day long;
> we are regarded as sheep to be slaughtered."

More mention of death. Yes, my father would know by now. I then moved to the glorious conclusion, which was filled with such richness and depth in this atmosphere of remembering a life well lived, in the midst of peace, acceptance, and faith. "No, in all these things we are more than conquerors through him who loved us. For I am sure that neither death nor life, nor angels nor rulers, nor things present nor things to come, nor powers, nor height nor depth, nor anything else in all creation, will be able to separate us from the love of God in Christ Jesus our Lord."

Would God not give us all things, knowing that he had already given us his Son? Nothing can separate us from the love of God in Christ Jesus, our Lord. What amazing assurance of a blessed conclusion. We prayed. Yes, we were held in that very moment by God's rich and solid assurance and love. The Holy Spirit—silent witness, real presence, strong comforter—was groaning with us.

We talked some more. My father needed some help with an impending bowel movement. We called a nurse, and I excused myself. In the hallway I ran into the female doctor who had been such a support in our meeting that afternoon. She asked me how my father was, and I reported on the option he was leaning toward. She was glad. She then showed me the coffee machine for visitors. What an excellent resource. Delicious real coffee. Blessed are the Dutch! I returned to my father, who had a very eventful day behind him. It was time for me to leave. We chatted a bit more and then hugged one another. Where and when would I next see him? On the way to the exit, I saw the female doctor again. We briefly chatted, and I was on my way. Turning to the highway, I saw that the vast blue skies had given way to dying light and increasing darkness. This had been a wonderful day in a bizarrely strange way. The inevitability of my father's death was there, but it was all held by something so vast and glorious. Or, better put, not something, but someone.

Hospice

The Wednesday Visit

WE SPOKE WITH MY FATHER ON A MONDAY EVENING, AND WE WERE worried things were going downhill fast. His speech had notably deteriorated, probably as a result of the painkillers he was receiving. We decided to visit him as soon as possible. Our youngest two had an "in service day" on the Wednesday, meaning they did not have school. My wife and three of our four children went to visit him in the hospice where he had been admitted a few days earlier. All this looked as if it were meant to be, both the place and the timing. My father had been in hospital for two weeks near the place where he lived. This had enabled neighbors, friends, and also his vicar to visit him on a number of occasions. It was a wonderful opportunity to say farewell to those who were living near. When my father had taken the decision not to have his leg amputated, the hospice option had come into view. In the Netherlands, a hospice is a place where everything is geared toward providing the best loving care in the closing days or weeks of a person's life. These places are run by professional nurses assisted by a substantial number of volunteers. The local GP visits regularly to oversee the medication (morphine) needs of the patients. Hospices provide the level of attention and care a busy hospital cannot give. This is a wonderful provision for many. We were very glad my father had decided for this option. Several of the hospices closer to my sister were full, but one place came available in a small hospice nearby. This was quite amazing, considering the long waiting lists in several other places. It felt like a miraculous provision. One was looking after my father. I had to think of John 14, where Jesus tells his disciples that he is going to prepare a place for them. That scripture had been in my mind as a possible second reading for my father's funeral, as well as for some other reasons we will come to.

This particular hospice had just six rooms, of which only three were in service, owing to COVID-19. The pandemic was on the way out but was still causing some havoc; hence many institutions were battling with staff shortages. The hospice was in a fairly quiet area outside the big city. A garden surrounded the building. There was pasture behind and a road and a modest moat in front. It was a pleasant place all around. What was located inside was even better, as we would discover. There were spacious rooms, a warm welcome, caring staff, and very helpful volunteers. When my father had entered the hospice, he had said about his grandchildren, "If they are not able to see me, tell them not to feel guilty; I love them all." At every step of the way, my father would think about other people affected by his new situation. As mentioned, my father's love and care were also illustrated by the money he had saved for each child over many years. What a generous gift—an inspiration!

Following the morning rush hour, we made our way to his new place. We traversed some highways I had driven on two weeks prior. There was a similar blue sky. We were still held and surrounded in glory. After the nearly three-hour journey, we arrived and parked the car. We could see him lying in bed on the ground floor. We felt my father was in the right place. He was not aware we were outside. My father was vision impaired for most of his life. He had no sight in one eye. On good days, he had 70 percent vision in the other. He looked small, but I was pleased that he was sitting upright and eating. We rang the bell. We were welcomed by a volunteer and went into the room, which was nice and spacious. There was a sitting area, and there were flowers on the coffee table. My father was very pleased to see everyone. He received serial hugs from the children, Janine, and me. He had grapes nearby, and he occasionally nibbled on one. I could see that his appetite was not as vigorous as when I last saw him in hospital. We had brought some things for his room. The best gift was a sizeable wooden heart, painted with the words "I love you" in bright colors by my youngest daughter of twelve. My father thought it was all very nice, but we realized he could not enjoy these things as he used to. He continued to nibble on the occasional grape. We all sat around the bed and in the seating area. There was the normal informality of a family gathering, with stories, bits of news, and tales of how school was going. One of my daughters working abroad called in, and she was able to see my father through video chat. He enjoyed speaking to her, but I could see it was a very difficult moment for her. When we sensed that my father was tired, we announced our departure. More serial hugs ensued. This felt like a significant moment for the children. This would be the last time they would see their grandfather alive. We drove off, making the long journey home.

The Saturday Visit

This time it was just Janine and me, just a few days later. On Friday night, we arrived in our apartment on the coast following rush-hour traffic. Originally, this weekend was earmarked for us to be away with our family to celebrate our thirtieth wedding anniversary. It all happened differently now. My eldest daughter had volunteered to look after her younger brother and sister. We could be away for a weekend together. I had no Sunday duties that week. It was perfect timing, as if it had to be this way. We dumped our stuff and went for a brief walk near the seafront. It was very windy. We returned and made ourselves a cup of tea. As we relaxed, we wondered how we would find my father.

We arrived at the hospice late Saturday morning. I was glad to see my sister and brother-in-law. We kissed and greeted my father and embraced them all. We had brought some flowers. Robert, one of the volunteers asked, "Do these stay?" For me this was ironic. It would have meant something different if my father had asked this question at home a few years prior. My father was never that keen on flowers. He would have to put them in a vase, add some water every couple of days, deal with petals that fell on the table, and eventually dispose of them and clean the vase—a small series of tasks for most of us, but for him a project or, better put, a series of projects. I explained this to Robert, who smiled. "I am not your father." With that statement and a twinkle in his eyes, he turned to prepare to put them in a vase. Robert came back with coffee and cake, a weekend treat for visitors. My sister and brother-in-law were on their way. We had time with my father. I noticed that he looked weaker than he had on Wednesday. I was so glad we took the children when we could. He was okay, but it was clear he was eating a lot less. There was no more nibbling of grapes. Morphine lessens one's appetite. He was quite a bit weaker now. He asked me again to have a good relationship with my sister. I assured him that this was what we all wanted. We prayed again, my hand on the folded hands of my father. He was completely at peace. There were no questions left, no doubt left. Just peace. I thanked him for the wonderful dad he had been and for the wonderful grandfather he had been. I had done this in the past, but it felt important to do it again to comfort and encourage my father with much love on this final stretch. My wife thanked him for the wonderful father-in-law he had been. He had been so accepting and welcoming from the very beginning until now. We stayed a bit longer and then said our farewells. He was getting very weak. How long would he last?

We returned to our place at the coast. We had a late lunch and later that afternoon went for a dive in the sea. People were in their winter gear on the beach, and we were in our swimsuits in the waves. Healthy oddballs, we are. "Refreshing" is probably the right word for that time of year. We love the sea any time of the year. We walked back over the boulevard, remembering the many times my father had visited us during the holidays. It always entailed the same sequence of events: picking him up from the nearby train station with one or more of the grandchildren, drinking coffee, unpacking the things he brought for us, having lunch (pretty much the same every time he came—his request), taking a walk on the seafront, and him treating us to ice cream. We have so many similar photos of similar moments over the years, with the children growing up and everyone gradually getting older. Blessed familiarity. Rhythms of bliss.

The Sunday Visit—Downhill

We woke to the sound of seagulls and sheep. Following our refreshing swim the day before, we had enjoyed a quiet evening. We had our breakfast and coffee and made our way to the hospice, which was just twenty minutes away. It was a quiet Sunday morning. It felt a bit strange for me not to take a church service. Again we felt provided and cared for. We drove to the hospice on this dry and windy day, making the now familiar journey. As we turned into the parking area, I saw that the window shades of my father's room were down. We rang the doorbell. A volunteer arrived, a serious look in her eyes. She invited us in and asked us to wait for a moment. One of the hospice staff came to inform us that things were going downhill rapidly for my father. We were being prepared. There was great stillness in the house. I opened the door and stepped into the room with Janine just behind me. My father was lying on his back, still. Mouth open. Dying. I felt shock but was sort of expecting this. He looked very different from how we had left him the previous day. The end was near.

Behind me I heard Janine crying. I turned around, but she was already being comforted by the lady who explained the latest developments to us. I proceeded to my father, kissed him on his face and forehead, and spoke to him. He felt colder than before. There was no response. He was alive, but I did not expect to see him with eyes open anymore. I had that sense the day prior when we said our good-byes. I was so glad for the moments we had with him the day before and on Wednesday, with the children. Next to his bed was a glass of water next to a stick with a small sponge on top of it. It reminded me of something: dying moments, suffering in its final stretch. A sacred remembering. Everything we wanted to say had been said. We had managed to say the thanks we wanted to say to him when he was still present. From the corner of my eye, I could see the bright painted heart with the assurance of love—solid love—on the windowsill. Janine came close, teary and red-eyed. We embraced. How precious it is to know her love. How precious it is to be loved. There was no way of knowing how long this would last. A few days, probably, but only God knew. My father's days were in his hands. We stayed with my father, drank coffee, held his hand, spoke to him, and prayed for him. We were met with silence. We made a quiet departure and took another long journey back, the image of him lying on his back, mouth open, etched on our minds.

The Last Wednesday Visit

Back home, the week had resumed its familiar rhythm: work, school, family meals. We woke up on Wednesday. The phone rang. I assumed it was probably the call we were dreading. Today was my sister's birthday. She was on the line. Immediately I realized something had happened. She had just been called. My father was in his final hour and might have died already.

They would get in the car immediately and hoped they would still catch him. I said I would come over as well but would not make any silly attempt to be there on time. We hastily said good-bye. I was going to text one of my uncles, who lived nearby. In the blur of the moment, with all the grief, haste, distraction, and precoffee clumsiness, I pushed the button to call. I got him on the phone straight away. I was a bit annoyed with myself, but I realized there are no accidents. He sounded very concerned. We promised to keep them informed. I gathered my things for the day. Janine lovingly prepared some things for me on the road: some sandwiches, just in case; the now familiar thermos of coffee; fruit; and water. Again I was on the road amid the rush-hour traffic, following the familiar route under the same blue skies. I knew I was not going to make it on time, but that was okay. We had said our farewells. I knew everything was well. It was well with his soul.

At the midway point, I stepped out of the car, stretched my legs, and did the necessary. It was a familiar relief. The sky was beautiful again, the air still cool. The sun was out, but its warmth was not yet evident. The tall grass was wet. I thought, "I am an earthling. Dust I am, and to dust I will return. Yet I know that 'the present day suffering does not compare to the glories that are to be revealed.'" I took a sip of coffee, breathing in the cool, pure air. Fields again stretched in front of me. Traffic sped on behind me. I got back in the car and drove on.

Traffic was not too bad. I was in deep thought. I knew I would not see my father alive anymore. Glory continued to be poured out. There was no need for speed. I progressed but was not there. At some point I realized I had missed a turn and did not quite realize where I was or where I had gone wrong. I returned to the present. I realized where I was and knew where I had to turn off. My detour took a bit longer, but no one would notice.

I arrived at the hospice from the opposite direction of that which I normally arrived from. The curtains of my father's room were closed. I knew his body was there, his life having left. I assumed they probably would be busy with him. I parked the car. In the distance, I saw my sister and brother-in-law through the windows of a separate building. I had wondered about the purpose of that building. Now I knew. This is where families gathered when their loved ones died.

We embraced. There was sadness, but there was also relief. My father had suffered to some extent, but no longer. My father's youngest brother and his wife, my uncle and aunt, the ones who live nearby, had decided to come following my accidental call. That was wonderful. They had been very kind to my father (and to us). It was special to have them with us at this moment. A volunteer asked whether we could use some coffee. Yes please! We were thankful for such wonderful people and provisions. My sister told me that when they got the call in the morning, they had stepped into the car immediately. The lady who was with my father when he breathed his last thought that he had passed away already, and she said so to my sister, but then there was one last shudder in my father, almost acknowledging the arrival of my sister. And then he was gone. My sister explained that a few people from the hospice were washing my father and clothing him. We had discussed what he would wear. What a birthday for my sister.

We had plenty of time before the funeral director would arrive. My sister and I exchanged memories about my father and mother. We discussed practical details. I informed the vicar, and we started to think about a possible day and time for the funeral. Were the vicar and church going to be free? What about the cemetery? There were so many things to investigate. It would all be all right. Things had been falling into place so well for so long now. This final stretch would be fine too. Some more calls were made. Some emails were sent. The funeral director from my father's village, just around the corner from where he lived, would arrive in an hour or so. We talked about my father and his last days, weeks, months, and years. My uncle was tearful. I am so glad he was there with my aunt. We waited. More calls were made. Various things were set in motion. Sandwiches arrived, as did more coffee. We were looked after so well and so lovingly. Things were happening. Our minds were active and busy. Our souls were not quite in sync—at least that is how it felt for me. It was all a mental and spiritual blur. I was going with the flow for most of it. My brother-in-law had to leave for a moment, and my uncle and aunt would soon be away for a short while as well.

After a while, a newish dark van turned into the parking area. This was the moment we had been waiting for. The funeral directors stepped out. A lean, tall man in his early sixties in a light gray suit and a shorter, plumper woman, a bit younger, in dark gray stepped out. We went outside and shook hands. No, they did not live in my father's village, but nearby.

The tall man in charge, who had driven the van, said he was one of the organists in the village church. If the regular organist would not play, we might have him for the service as well. They were friendly and professional. They were here for a reason and would need to be back on the road. They were certainly not in a rush, but things were moving forward. A brand-new coffin was retrieved from the van and put on the trolley they brought. My sister and I had chosen the coffin from a website a few days earlier. It was all a bit surreal. With the empty coffin on the trolley, they made their way toward my father's room to meet with hospice staff. We would be called.

My uncle and aunt had been away but could join us for this last part of the proceedings. Also my brother-in-law was back. We were all invited to enter the room. There my father lay. Thin. Gaunt. He was wearing a familiar set of gray pants, a shirt and tie, and a homely green vest. No suit—that would not have been him. Yes, this was my father, but all life was gone. Just his thin, pale, worn-out body remained. I remembered other dead family members—my mother, my grandparents—in years gone by. My father looked neat and tidy. We stood for a moment in silence. The lady from the hospice welcomed us and explained how things had evolved over the past twenty-four hours and what had happened during the night. She explained that someone had been with my father when he breathed his last, and that he had been at peace. The funeral director took over and explained what would happen next. We were given the option to carry my father's body into the coffin. We looked at each other, and my brother-in-law and I were willing to assist. We were instructed how to do it. I placed my hands underneath my father's shoulders and was close to his face. As expected, his body was very stiff. We lifted him up. He was not that heavy. It was a profound moment. I was so thankful for this opportunity. This ordinary act that needed to happen took on deep intimacy and significance. We placed him in the coffin, which was made of oak with a light color, simple yet beautiful. The craftsmanship of the wooden vessel caused me to remember my father's father and his creative skills. We mentioned the infected leg to the funeral director, feeling that he should know. The lady of the hospice explained how they had prepared it. The funeral director expressed appreciation for how my father's body had been prepared. Nods were made. A moment of professional courtesy blended with human respect and kindness.

The colorful painted heart bearing the message "I love you" was placed with my father in the coffin. It would be placed on top during the funeral service. We had discussed the details with our youngest daughter. I felt the need to pray. I asked whether this was okay for everyone, and we took our places around the coffin. We closed our eyes. I could feel grief welling up, but in this moment, I could not allow it to take over, for now. That would be for later. I felt weak, yet I felt strong. Is that not what St. Paul said? I prayed, thanking God for my father, his life, his love, and his care. I thanked God for his wonderful provisions of people and places, as well as for the loving care my father had received in the place where we were. It was such a special place. I asked for God's comfort and strength in the days to come. We all needed it. It was a simple prayer. God was there. I knew he was there. He had been there all the time. The peace my father experienced in this last stretch of his life had indeed been beyond all understanding. My father had died completely at peace, well looked after from above and below.

The lady from the hospice was pleasantly surprised. She had never experienced something like that at this point in the proceedings. She had, however, prepared something as well. It was our turn to be surprised. My sister, brother-in-law, and I were invited to do the honors of closing the coffin. The coffin was closed for now. The formal closing would take place just before the funeral. A beautiful quilted blanket was placed over it. My father's coffin was wheeled out of his room, which had become such a special place for us. We turned just left and placed my father at the center of the building, on the center of the cross that divided the different parts of the ground floor. A large glass jar stood on a pedestal. It contained a solid crème-colored candle which was lit. Around it were dried flower petals and leaves. They were from the garden of the hospice, the lady explained. It looked beautiful. She said the candle would remain burning till the funeral of my father had taken place, and she smiled at us. I was deeply touched at their thought and care. What an inspiration. It was a testimony of love.

Volunteers and staff were waiting to gather around the coffin. The lady spoke a few words and mentioned how everyone had so enjoyed my father. I was not surprised, but it felt good to hear it noted. She then explained the tradition of the house. A volunteer read a poem. A moment of silence was kept. My father was remembered. Here we were, with strangers-no-longer, who stood with us and were our comfort, in a moment of human dignity and sharing—a holy pause. A warm blanket was covering our grief and the coffin.

The special, brief holy moment then came to an end. Space was made around the coffin. The funeral staff took over. The coffin was wheeled to the dark gray van outside for a last moment of farewell. The beautiful blanket was folded and returned to the house. The coffin slid into the van. My hand was on the coffin. I had felt coffins in cars and vans on numerous occasions, presiding at funerals. Now it was my father's moment to make this journey. A flower from a bunch of flowers given by my mother-in-law was placed on the coffin. My father was ready to return home or, well, very close to it. The lady explained to the funeral director how she would like things to happen. The funeral staff nodded. We said our farewells and wished them a smooth journey. They greeted us politely, and the man stepped into the van. The funeral lady took her place in the front of the van, and when her colleague was ready, she started to walk slowly toward the road. Traffic stopped. She and the van, a few meters behind her, turned right onto the road. She slowly walked away from the home. We soon could see them no longer. A mischievous part of me wondered how long they would keep this up. I knew that at the boundary of the hospice grounds, the lady would step into the van and they would be on their way, probably chatting about what had happened. Maybe, maybe not. We turned aside, thanked the staff for their love and care, and prepared to gather our belongings to be on our way.

My sister kindly offered a meal, but because of the driving I still had to do, I thankfully declined. I would make a quick visit to my mother-in-law, who lived nearby. I called her to ask whether it was okay to drop by. It was. It was good to see her and to tell her what had happened. I told her about one of her flowers travelling with my father. She asked me why I had not used the whole bunch, to which I did not have a clear answer. The story of my life?

We ate a quick sandwich, and I was on my way again. It all reminded me of my drive back from the hospital months prior. Glorious daylight faded, and the evening darkness was soon all around. Again I was by myself in the car, but this felt different. Now I was without my father in a bed somewhere. I was thinking of his body. I knew where it was. I felt emptiness, loss. I needed to focus and get home safely.

In Between

A Blur

THE DAYS BETWEEN DEATH AND FUNERAL WERE A BIT OF A BLUR. Tiredness from going back and forth during the past few weeks was catching up with all of us. At the same time, there was no time to rest, but we had to. I removed as many obligations from my diary as possible, clearing the deck. I needed space. *Think. Pray. Wait.*

In-between times are important. They give us time to make transitions. They help us to catch up with reality. They help us to sort through things and thoughts. We needed time to get ready. There were so many things to organize. A division of labor appeared quite naturally. My sister focused on the necessary and immediate tasks, such as writing the card and getting the news out. Fortunately my sister had started the list of people who needed to know when my father was still at home. That made for a wonderful head start. The recent death of her mother-in-law had helped her to get ready for this moment too. After a bit of back-and-forth about the text on the card, we were there. The card's heading would read, "Nothing can separate us from the love of God," a summary phrase for the end of Romans 8, such an important text for my parents. The hope my father had asked for was already making its way into the world. Then there were the arrangements with the funeral home, the church service, and the burial. There were so many details to work out: time, place, mode of transport, people involved. It was important for all these things to be thought about so that on the day things could flow and everyone would be able to focus on what truly matters.

I started to work on elements of my father's funeral service. The readings were clear now. They had emerged over the last few weeks. The pinnacle ending of Romans 8 had appeared very clearly as one of the texts. The other reading came from the beginning of John 14, where Jesus tries to prepare his disciples for his imminent departure. This text resonated for various reasons. Jesus was thinking about those who would be left behind, something my father had been doing as well. "Rooms prepared" with forethought and generosity was another important theme; it related to the welcomes my father had received in many family homes over the years, as well as the places prepared for him in the closing weeks of his life. This text, not unusual for funerals, had come to me specifically when the place in the hospice materialized. Then, of course, that was the great assurance for all of us left behind—that Jesus went away to prepare a place in his fathers' home, and that he will be back. I knew this was certainly important for a number of us, and I hoped that the generosity of that promise would bless and intrigue every person present in the church. Finally there were Thomas and Philip, who were hesitant to accept the reality of Jesus's announced departure. To some extent, that could reflect on us, but I was thinking more of the doubting and questioning by Thomas and Philip that had also characterized stretches of my father's journey. Their questioning and doubting were graciously addressed and, in due course, resolved, as was the case for my father.

I had some ideas about hymns, but that took a bit longer to become clear. The starting point was the closing hymn of my mother's funeral, "Thine Be the Glory," from a French hymn which often is a centerpiece on Easter morning, declaring with joy and boldness the resurrection of our Lord. This would be the closing hymn in my father's funeral service as well. I can still see the closing part of my mother's funeral service, with her coffin being carried out of the church door as light flooded back into church. Death will not have the last word. Life will. Other hymns chosen all expressed hope in the God who has conquered death and who will make all things new—the One, who brings comfort and hope in the midst of grief and despair. A bit more on the hymns later.

It was very good to work together with my father's vicar. She had been very kind in visiting my father till the very end. She even offered to go to the hospice in my father's dying days, driving more than an hour away, but I dissuaded her. My father was already too far away at that point, but we greatly valued her love and care for him over the last years. We met on

Zoom, which was such a convenience. We had intended to do that a few weeks earlier than we did, but life had been too busy. It did not matter. Things clicked. She would lead the service and would do the burial. I would preach and would arrange for people to read and for our family to do part of the prayers. We discussed the hymns and how and when they would be played and sung.

Sermon preparation progressed in remarkable fashion. My father had died on Wednesday morning, and on Friday morning the entire sermon came to me. Ideas had been simmering over the last few weeks. It now had to be downloaded on paper. It all happened in one sitting. I preach on most weeks, and normally there is quite a bit of writing, rewriting, and editing to do. This time it basically was writing only. Edits over the days that followed were minimal. I find it extraordinary as I think back on it. I so felt divine inspiration and the "peace that surpassed all understanding"—a presence I would also feel on the day of the funeral. Over the days that followed, things started to fall further into place: the people who would say something about Dad and Granddad, the people who would do the readings, the people who would pray. An order of service emerged. Checked. Blessed. Printed.

That Sunday, we received some bad news. Our daughter who lived and worked in the UK was not able to come for reasons of ill health. This was a difficult situation for all of us. This was something that needed to be worked through after the funeral. We decided to look for a hotel to make our journey to the funeral less stressful. We all thought about what to wear and what not to wear. It was all coming together.

On Monday evening after school and dinner, we got in the car and drove off. It was late when we arrived in our hotel.

Nearly Home

Hotel

HOME. HOSPITAL. HOSPICE. HOTEL. EACH WAS ANOTHER STEP ALONG the way. We had all slept quite well. Because the funeral had to start at a particular time in the morning, we had decided to avoid the morning rush-hour stress by staying in a hotel nearby. This turned out to be a good decision. The early morning was dark and damp. There were probably traffic problems everywhere. Actually, we love our hotel stays as a family. They offer the great pleasure of something different. The hotel breakfast, especially, is a reason for anticipation and joy. The hotel was on the edge of the woods, a few kilometers north of my home village. When we entered the hotel the night prior, I knew I had been in this place before. Roughly forty years ago, a friend and I had stayed in a camper nearby, preparing for our exams in the daytime, and playing billiards and drinking beer in the evening. The billiards table was still there. On this visit, the staff were friendly and even helped me with a weird request. Having brought a different bag from the one I normally travel with, I realized that I had not brought a clerical board. This was not a disaster, but it was something to fix if we could. An improvised strip of cut out white cardboard did the job.

After our showers and dressing up, we were ready for our breakfast. The excitement of a hotel stay mixed with the solemnity of what was coming. One by one, the family assembled downstairs in the breakfast area. There was delicious bread and good coffee. It was so good to be back in the Netherlands. There was sadness at this special family moment. One of us was missing. One of my daughters had not been able to come at the last minute. We missed her. Then there was the reason for our journey—to say farewell to a wonderful dad, father-in-law, and grandfather. How would that be? Would we manage to do our bits well? We exchanged some stories and kept an eye on the clock. We then all made our way back to our rooms for final packing and brushing of teeth. When I did a final run-through of the rooms, I found my white stole dropped on the floor. I was glad to have found it. We drove off, the darkness and dampness slowly lifting.

From the edge of the forest, we drove through the town, making a straight journey south toward our village. It all seemed so much smaller than I remembered. This was the place where I had gone to school, where I had taken my music lessons, where we had gone shopping on Saturdays with the smell of warm sausage in the department store, and where we had had our school Christmas concerts in the church in the town center. These are precious memories.

Our journey was short and simple. I had to think back to a girl from my school who lived just off this road to the left. I had helped her with math on a few occasions and had been madly in love with her in year four. I had declared my love to her and showered her with gifts and attention. My exuberance had not met with joyful acceptance. Maybe I had been a bit too enthusiastic. It clearly was not meant to be. I wondered what happened to her. I put a hand on the leg of my soulmate in the passenger seat. I had to smile about my youthful passion and folly.

The road we drove on had various familiar stretches, but it had changed dramatically in certain places. The train station, for example, I think is now in its third major rebuild since I left home. The road used to cross the tracks fifty years ago. Now everything had disappeared underground. The bus station had been moved to the other side of the tracks many years ago. An old factory just south of the tracks, which once suffered a series of gas explosions on a fateful evening when we were young, had now disappeared. I can still remember watching the strange glows and lights in the night sky from our loft window. Bits of ancient wood bordering the tracks on the south side as well had now been cleared for apartments, houses, and offices. Everything changes.

It was another beautiful day in the making. Things were still a bit damp, but the skies were clearing. The road entering the village was glorious. Stately ancient trees in autumnal dress greeted us solemnly. We passed the place where my father's body had resided for the last few days on our left. The funeral home was part of a large chain. I remembered the funeral director who had started the company fifty years ago. His son and I were in the same class in primary school. One day we were detained into our lunch hour because the class had not behaved well. There was a certain injustice to all this, as only a few boys had been the problem (Mr. Innocent not included!). Fifteen minutes into our detention, a black Mercedes stopped in front of the school. A portly man with a very red head stepped out. A sharp brief conversation with the teacher took place, and we were all liberated. The fact that our case was made by a professional who had spare empty coffins at his disposal must have added weight to the argument, or so I like to think. Many years ago, his company had been bought out by the large chain. The people we had met a few days before had been kind, but they were somewhat anonymous, nameless. I wondered what happened to my classmate. Shortly after passing the funeral home, we passed the lane where my father lived. We had decided not to go to the house today but to instead focus all our attention and emotional energy on church and the cemetery.

Back in Church

We drove toward the church in the center of the village. We proceeded carefully. The village center had been made pedestrian- and cycle-friendly. I had so many memories on these streets. We turned into the parking area. There were plenty of places left. We parked and got out. A man in a suit walked toward us. He was with the funeral home and pointed to the reserved spot he had guarded for us. We thanked him but decided to stay where we were. We got our stuff and made our way to the church hall. We entered and in a side room saw the coffin. I went over and looked at my father's body for a moment. I would be back soon to close his coffin with my sister and her husband. We were led to a large room and were offered coffee—a Dutch life essential, as you must realize by now. We put our things down and made our way to the church. We were greeted by the lady from the funeral home, who was in charge. She was professional and friendly. All preparations had gone well. There was so much to think about, and there were plenty of details to discuss before the service, but there was no major stress, and everything happened gently and in good harmony.

The last time we had been in this church was for my mother's funeral nearly thirty years before. At various points, memories of that day drifted in. So much had happened in those thirty years. Grandchildren were born and had grown to adulthood. The youngest was twelve. The eldest was twenty-two. My sister and her family had built up her life in the city where she had studied. Janine and I had spent most of those thirty years abroad. My father had always worshipped at this church for as long as he lived here. He had even served as an elder for several years. Every church community knows ups and downs, but this church had been marked by a certain constancy in its faithfulness and care. On this day, we were very aware of that.

The church had been renovated beautifully. The floor was made up of large gray stone slabs instead of the bare wooden floorboards I remembered. I assumed a heating system had been installed underground. The pews had all been sanded, and the massive round heating pipes had been taken out. As a result, the entrance to the pews had gone to ground level, instead of the old situation where you had to step into the pews. There also appeared to be more space between the pews. The ancient gravestones at the back of church had been beautifully preserved. There was even one section of glass floor to show the ancient foundation walls of the earlier church. It was all done well. The blue and yellow rose window against the white wall above the pulpit provided a focal point of pure beauty. How precious it was to be back, and how profound it was to say farewell to my father in this special place of beauty and memories. The microphone and lectern were tested by the people doing readings and prayers. Some last-minute discussions took place on where everyone would sit. All was well.

Family members gradually arrived. It was very good to see everyone. All of them with their own stories of bereavement and (health) challenges. My father's family was marked by great harmony. He had three brothers and one sister, all married with children. My father was the eldest. His passing was a marker for his generation. Throughout the years, these brothers, sister, and their spouses had consistently met for birthdays and other family high days. Often my father was picked up or was invited to stay over. He was grateful for the invitations but mostly appreciated his own bed. As a result, the sleepovers had gradually diminished over the years. I had been impressed with the love and harmony between these siblings. What is it that makes some families dwell in love and friendship, while others are splintered by strife and ill-feeling? This is complex stuff.

A few of us went to close my father's coffin: my sister, my brother-in-law (we had done this bit at the hospice as well) and the funeral director. To my surprise, my youngest daughter (twelve) wanted to be present as well. Before the lid was closed, she asked me whether the wooden heart she had painted for her grandfather ("*Opa,*" as she referred to him) could stay with him in the coffin (as it had done on the way from the hospice to the funeral home). That was possible, and the bright painted heart with "I love you" on it was placed on the folded hands of my father. Nothing can separate us from God's love, and this expression very much looked like the incarnate type. We closed the lid. There was a moment of silence and stillness. Again that blend of normality and reverence. The coffin was prepared to be rolled into church. We still had some time before the service would start.

When we came back into the reception room, the vicar had arrived and was making the rounds with the family. She also warmly greeted us. We discussed the final details for the service. We then began to get ready to start the service. Cassocks were put on. Bibles, liturgies, and sermon notes were checked. We started to line up to exit the church hall to go around the church to enter from the main door in front. The grandchildren would pull the trolley with my father's coffin toward the main entrance. It was wonderful to see them doing this together. Pillars. Olive shoots around your coffin, as the Psalmist would have described the scene.

We slowly made our way outside were about to enter the church. It was a majestic moment. I was so glad to walk beside Janine, held on all sides. We entered. I felt sadness and solemnity as I saw familiar and unfamiliar faces. My father's coffin was placed in front of the church. Candles were lit by all his grandchildren present. The service started. The vicar led with warmth and calm dignity. It was good to sit in front with her, so I did have some time to get used to all who were in church. I felt emotion sinking in. If I had seen all these faces just before my preaching, it would have hit me harder. This was a tremendous help.

This hallowed place with so many memories from my youth was such a place of bliss and beauty. Yet we were here for a bittersweet and solemn task—to give thanks for a blessed life and to seek comfort with God and with one another. Family sat on the front rows and a bit further down in the church. I recognized neighbors old and new, as well as some friends of my sister's. I saw one of the doctors who had given such loving advice and compassion to my father in hospital. We smiled as recognition passed between us. I saw some other people from the village—some people I did not recognize. I turned to the right, where we used to sit as a family, always in the same section. Some neighbors and friends were sitting there now. There was an atmosphere of dignity, reverence, warmth, and gratitude—a wonderful blend. The Lord was with us. We knew gentle comfort, and all those who spoke were given the strength to do what they needed to do.

Our opening hymn, "For All the Saints Who from Their Labors Rest," is a majestic, long hymn—one you can sing when entering a large cathedral. According to Bible scholar Tom Wright, this is a hymn with flawless theology on death, dying, and resurrection—not a small feat. I just loved it for its profound blend of dignity and deep hope. Everything in this service was geared toward hope and life. From the welcome to the music, to the signing, to the spoken word, everything was drenched in gratitude and hope. I saw my father as he was before me. This was a true celebration of life.

My sister was the first to speak for the family. I felt for her. A bit nervous, she spoke more rapidly than normal. She gave a loving account of my father's life, including some lovely details about my father that we all recognized. The recollection made us smile. My sister had been so loving and faithful to my father. His death and her birthday were now linked forever. She accomplished her contribution of love—another act of service. Then came the grandchildren's turn. My eldest and youngest daughters, also the eldest and youngest grandchildren, were next. They lovingly shared memories about Opa's visits, ice cream, and precious visits to his place and to ours. Everyone was so thankful for the generous and kind man he had been.

We then listened to the organist improvising on a hymn we would sing after the readings. It was a beautiful reflective moment to let words spoken in love sink in. The readings followed, read by my aunt and a dear family friend. As I heard the words of Romans 8 and John 14, I remembered the various things that had happened over the last few weeks. I thought of my tired and unshaven father in his large hospital bed and light blue pajamas, the rooms prepared by a loving Lord, the request for hope …

We sang "Er is een land van louter licht" (based on "There Is a Land of Pure Light"; see appendix B). This is a beautiful hymn drenched in resurrection hope. We had sung it at my mother's funeral. The familiar words and music take us to a promised land of delight where there are no longer tears and death, separation, darkness, or suffering. There is honesty about doubt and fear, yet light and hope prevail. We are encouraged for our journey home.

It was time for me to speak. Following is the transcript of my sermon:

Good singing….! :-)

Evelyne and I remembered on the day our father died that my father could always sing with abandon in this church....

We always sat in that block [pointing to the right] of the church....never anywhere else.........

......and my father could sing well loudly.... sometimes skipping....and then a poke from my mother....Great memories.....

A few times my father and I had discussed his funeral..... but everything came into focus almost four weeks ago....

After a very good conversation with his caring and patient doctors, my father had come to the conclusion that he no longer wanted an amputation of his leg.....and that the final phase of his life had begun....

He knew he would not return to his home....

He was sorry it would end this way... but he was at peace with it..... I was full of admiration....

Dad asked Evelyne and me to arrange and take care of various things.... definitely not controlling...but caring

He was often concerned with the time he would be gone.....and thought of those who would be left behind....

Kind, generous...and above all very practical.....

It was a significant moment.... my father quietly in bed....in familiar pyjamas ....

my dear father so diminished by illness over the years.... but so characteristically my father....

Outside....a beautiful blue sky....and sunshine.....and a big Acacia tree....

God had given a piece of Acacia Lane with him.... :-)

Then Dad quietly asked if I could contact Reverend Verbaan ....who he appreciated so much....to ask her to lead his service.....and he asked me to preach....

"Paul ....can you choose readings that give hope....."...... always thinking of others.....

So here we are....

Everything went fast anyway...but not too fast....

We had time for everything....and we took our time......

Fantastic care in Ede...and in the hospice in Sassenheim.... spots reserved for him..... it had to be so....

With incredibly kind, warm, patient, caring people....

We are very grateful for the care my father received....

'Nothing can separate us from the love of God....'

The brief summary of the end of Romans 8.... my parents' wedding text....also on dad's card......

And one of our readings this morning

His parents' wedding and death text in Romans 14 would also have been very nice....

"None of us lives for himself, and none of us dies for himself. As long as we live, we live for the Lord; and when we die, we die for the Lord. So whether we live or die, we belong to the Lord."

This is also a text my father lived....

But on that afternoon I read this piece from Romans 8.... but I started a little earlier....

.......In a piece that deals with suffering....v18

"I am convinced that the suffering of this time is out of all proportion to the glory that will be revealed to us in the future."

I watched my father...with his incurably ill leg in familiar pyjamas .....listening intently in his bed...sitting.... lightly nodding.....

.....and a bit further....

"For creation is prey to futility".....think of disease... wars....and death....

and then we read these simple words...But there is hope..."

BUT THERE IS HOPE!......

"....... we sigh within ourselves awaiting the revelation that we are children of God: the redemption of our mortal existence.....in this HOPE we are saved!"

This was what my father hoped for.....

My father KNEW he was a child of God....

And why could he trust that?

And why can we rely on that....?

Because God loves us... All of us....!!!

"If God is for us, who can be against us?

Will He, who did not spare His own Son, but gave Him up for the sake of us all, not also with Him give us everything?"

NOTHING can separate us from the love of God.....

He who did not spare His own Son....

The Son....Jesus.....who is busy encouraging those left behind....

Jesus...busy preparing ....for when he would no longer be here....

When I read this section in John 14.... I see things from disciples of Jesus, Thomas and Philip (who comes a little later in the chapter) in pa........and also from Jesus.....

Let's start with the disciples of Jesus....

The disciples are not wildly enthusiastic about change....

Even when someone tells them that a wonderful lodging place has been arranged for them.... :-)

Over the years...after my mother passed away... several family members here..... had my father as a lodger. Normally 1 or 2 nights.

For weeks the phone conversations went on about whether he should do it or not...he did not look forward to it :-)

And then when he had been....it was always very nice after all....

Thanks to everyone here who so lovingly and patiently went through all that......throughout the years...... numerous times....

My father was not wildly enthusiastic about change.... and that was true for as long as I knew him....

Dad also specifically had a thing about THOMAS

Doubting Thomas...as he is still known.....

Thomas asking questions....(nothing wrong with questions by the way!!)

Thomas who for a few days cannot believe the news... that Jesus has risen from the dead.....

Thomas who of course does eventually cry out ... My Lord and my God!!........but that only came for Thomas at the end....

....or should I say.....the end of the beginning.... ?

My father had his doubts...over the years....

He kept finding it hard that he lost my mother....his Jeanne....to death so early....

Why? ....I heard that question so many times....

And there were also other questions and doubts...... which we had had over the years..... and that's normal....... and asking questions is good....

But dad also had something from JESUS...in John 14....

Jesus....who in love and care prepared things.... for those who would be left behind......

Evelyne and I know how many things Dad took good care of....

But also caring for others....when he went into hospice...about the grandchildren: "If someone doesn't have the chance to see me.... it doesn't matter.... I love them all..."

What struck me these last weeks....was that at the end of his life..... protestation Philip and doubting Thomas had all fallen away .....and only the peace of Jesus remained....

Not a trace of doubt.... anymore

Not a trace of rebellion....or struggle.....anymore

The last times we were together and spoke..... in what would become his deathbed.... Talking together....and praying....hands folded on the blankets....

Very simple.... not many words.....simple..... trusting...

Just peace.... the peace that passes all understanding....

The peace we can all know through Jesus.... who called himself the Way....the Truth and the Life.... to give comfort and assurance to those who would be left behind....

Jesus.... who conquered death.....

He is the HOPE that all futility.... disease....war.... violence.... will come to an end......

Dear friends.... brothers and sisters.....We are here together in gratitude and hope.....For nothing can separate us from the love of God.....

My father knew how true that was when he came to the end of his life...That's why he could be so calm....

How did my father experience that love of God....?

Sometimes God's love comes directly.....

Walking in nature...or in a church service.... that you become so filled with God's love.... that you want to sing loudly.....sometimes a bit too loudly..

I hope everyone here this morning can feel that love in this service....because God's love is for everyone!.....[also those who follow this via the internet]

Directly is beautiful..... but often God's love comes through others....

Like today........Finding comfort and hope with each other.....

Sharing beautiful and funny memories......

And..spoiler alert.....Over a cup of coffee....and a sausage roll .... my father would have been so happy....

God's love also comes through others.....I already mentioned the good care my father received...in hospital and hospice....

God's love through pastor or elder or someone from the church visiting....

For years we sat in that block of the church to hear where the flowers are going that Sunday...and then the day comes when you hear that the flowers are going to your father.... very beautiful

God's love through wonderful neighbors and friends who all took care of my father... over the years

Messages.... mail..... meals.... so sweet and faithful

So nice that we were still able to celebrate on his 85th birthday at Panorama hoeve....

God's love through family....Beautiful to see....how through the many years....brothers and sisters got along.....

God's love through children and grandchildren....

Very grateful also to Evelyne...Paul and children.... how you were always there for dad.... especially when we lived further away....

We live in what so often seems like a senseless world.... illness.... good-bye..... grief.....

We live in an uncertain world.....wars....threat....

BUT THERE IS HOPE..... !!

BECAUSE:.......We also live in a world where love so often already triumphs....

And eventually love will completely overcome... I believe......

Where light shines....darkness gives way....

Will he who has not spared his Son give us WITH HIM....not all things?

NOTHING can separate us....from the LOVE......
of GOD.....

Absolutely nothing..... AMEN

I sat sound and felt profound gratitude. Prayers
followed. We prayed our gratitude and we sang it once
more:

Now thank we all our God
with heart and hands and voices,
who wondrous things has done,
in whom his world rejoices;
who from our mothers' arms
has blessed us on our way
with countless gifts of love,
and still is ours today.

How true are those words, each and every one of them!

The service in church was drawing to a close. The service was concluded
with "Thine Be the Glory," A great hymn celebrating the resurrection. This
is a defiant, victorious hymn we normally sing on Easter morning. Originally
a French hymn, we have sung it in various languages in the various countries
we have lived in. Different languages, same hope. Death will not have the
last word. Hope and life will. This also had been the closing hymn for my
mother's funeral. As I said, I can still see her coffin being carried out of the
church by six men in dark gray, with light flooding back in. I still feel the
powerful and potent mix of sadness and profound hope and joy.

The Last Stretch

With the life-filled notes of "Thine be the Glory" ringing in our ears,
my father's coffin started to make the last part of the journey. The
grandchildren again were leading the coffin on its way. We came out of
the main church doors on the main street, turned right, and turned right
again around the church toward the cemetery. Traffic stopped. We crossed
a road and entered the first section of the cemetery.

Heaven

Home. Hospital. Hospice. Hotel. Heaven. The weather had turned stunningly beautiful. The damp darkness of the early morning had entirely lifted. The blue heavens that had accompanied us over the past few weeks again greeted us, embracing everything and holding everything. The trees around the cemetery were immensely beautiful. I have never seen such a perfect Autumn day. As we were on our way, the glorious skies again reminded us of the glories to be revealed. We crossed a second road to enter the last section of the cemetery, where my mother was buried. As I read the familiar stones as we went along, some stories of families came back to me. I saw the grave of a younger sister of a classmate in primary school. She had coped with various illnesses in her youth and had died at a young age. We then passed a section with child graves, many of them very colorful. Some were very pink. Some tragic stories came back to mind. Everything was held in tremendous beauty.

The Very Last Stretch

The grandchildren, my brother-in-law, and I were carrying the coffin from the trolley to the grave, the very last bit of his journey. People were spread around on the path and on the grass, sadness and reverence on faces. Carried by the love of so many, my father's body was brought to his final resting place. Again we remembered that day when my mother was buried in the same grave.

In the midst of this solemnity, something funny happened. Our youngest daughter was at the very back of the carrying team, her view obscured by the taller grandchildren. Just in front of the open grave was a small mound of earth and small scoop, brand-new. My daughter had not heard the soft warning from the funeral director, and she could not see anything anyway. As we were making the turn toward the grave she kicked the scoop into the open grave. Oops. I watched the face of the gravedigger standing in the corner on the side. A suppressed expression of sadness about the sudden loss of this useful implement passed across his face and his eyes, as if he were thinking, "That was such a nice scoop." He held the rest of his composure perfectly. The coffin was lowered all the way. I could see part of the scoop peeping out below the coffin. I was wondering whether the sad gravedigger was going to attempt to retrieve it. My guess was yes, but I felt no need to find out. I can live with loose ends and mystery.

We turned our attention from the buried scoop and lowered coffin to the vicar. Words of assurance and blessing met our ears. We were reminded that all tears will be wiped away, a new heaven and a new earth will come, death will be no more, and God will live with his people forever. *Yes, Lord, we believe*! I thought. *Thank you for being with us in our grief. Thank you for the people you gave to my father. Thank you for the comfort we receive this very moment.*

A last prayer ensued, and we were then invited to take a bit of soil and throw it on the coffin. We took some moments to remember my father. Dust to dust. We slowly turned back to the church, followed by others who had shown their last respects. My father was loved by many. We made our way back past the stones bearing the familiar names. Their stories are known, some of them by us. We crossed the road and reentered the first part of the cemetery, once again with gravel grinding beneath our shoes. We then crossed the final road. We were almost back in the church. An immense acacia was greeting us from the back of the church. I was home again away from home.

I returned to the vestry. The vicar joined us and gave Janine a big hug in a moment of shared humanity, shared experiences, deep compassion, and warmth. We thanked her for a wonderful, warm service. Mission accomplished. We were thankful; empty, but still carried.

Sausage Rolls and Coffee

We entered the church hall. Again this was a place with many childhood memories: evenings at the village chess club, youth groups on Sundays, the annual church fair. I had spent so many hours here. I remembered an Easter breakfast we once participated in—orange juice and boiled eggs for the masses.

Yellow daffodils stood on the table, proclaiming resurrection's victory. The hall had also seen renovation but still had the familiar atmosphere of warmth and welcome. Lots of people had joined us. Photos of family moments were displayed on the wall. It was wonderful to see these very familiar photos. Some had not been seen for so many years, a feast of recognition. Coffee, sausage rolls, wraps, and pastries were served in abundance. Especially the combination of coffee and sausage rolls would have pleased my father. There were animated conversations around the tables. Images of my father at various stages in his life were the backdrop of our noisy gathering. This was a foretaste of heaven.

My sister, her husband, I, and Janine were lined up to greet people and receive their condolences. There were several people I did not know, including a few of my father's old colleagues. I found this quite amazing, considering he had retired more than twenty years before. One female colleague, a staunch spinster decades ago, was now happily married. We both remembered how we as a family had visited her parents' farm one Sunday afternoon. My sister had stepped in a massive cow dropping, and I was tasked with bringing the cows in for milking, by wearing her father's cap. I also remembered the farm's "state room," with immaculate furniture, plates, and cutlery, to be briefly visited and admired only. I asked her whether that room was still there. Of course it was! She was somewhat surprised by my strange question. Another colleague introduced himself. He had shared an office with my father. At that time, my father had been coming to the end of his working life, and this man had just been at the beginning of his own. He had fond memories of my father. There were lots of family, neighbors, and friends, some of them now very old. There were also some remote family members whom I did not know or was not aware of at all. Additionally, there were some friends of my sister who had also been there for my mother's funeral. One of these friends, now prominent in the legal profession, I remembered as a pudgy teenager. She was now a determined professional woman. Having recently come across a book by her father or grandfather, I found it great to talk to her briefly. It was wonderful to share stories and memories with those who were there. There was plenty of joy.

When the end of the line came into view, one more person arrived. I had not seen him in the service. He gave his condolences and mentioned that he had been unable to attend the service, as he had been at work. He had been my father's barber. He told me that over many years he had cut the (ever thinning) hair of my father and that they often had discussed faith. My father had expressed his doubts, and the friendly man behind him had offered his assurance while snipping away at my father's thin white locks. I shared with him how peacefully my father had died. Afterward we were in email contact, and I sent him the order of service and sermon notes. He was a partner in a good ending.

The doctor who attended the service, and who was a member of this church community, also came to say farewell. She said how touched she was by the service and the mention of our conversation in the hospital. More people started to leave. We said farewell. We had some time together as immediate family, and then it was time for everyone to head home. Everybody was getting ready for their journeys. We said farewell to my uncle, who had lost his wife more than a year before. His son-in-law would drive him to catch up with a study tour on Chagall church windows in France. It would be the trip where he would meet a widow and new love would blossom.

The ladies from church who had organized the reception had boxed up all the leftover sandwiches, wraps, and pastries. We would not go hungry for many days. There was also a box for the funeral director. There was so much. The catering was generous, having been planned with a mindset of better safe than sorry.

All went well. This day had been rich, yet normal; so intense and yet so peaceful and almost relaxed. It was strange and beautiful. It would take me a while to let everything sink in. It had been a beautiful homecoming. We departed still in autumn glory. Darkness set in as we were on the highway. My father was home.

The Days After

Day with My Sister

I EMBARKED ON ANOTHER LONG CAR JOURNEY TO MY FATHER'S HOUSE. IT was another beautiful day. Leaving after the rush hour traffic, my aim was to arrive around midday, have some lunch with my sister, and then sort through various things in the afternoon. I arrived as planned and parked the car—this time in front of the drive, to make the loading up of the car later a bit easier.

I suddenly remembered how I had first arrived at the house in the summer of 1970. I was nearly six years old. The move had been a big adventure. My father had been in the hospital for an eye operation. We did not have a car yet, so we were driving in the van with the movers. I remembered the "head mover," a big, burly man. Strangely, I remembered what he had for lunch en route—meatballs with gravy on white bread, which had struck me as extravagant at the time. The human ability to remember trivia seems unending. Later I discovered that this man lived just a few streets away from us. We would bump into him every so often.

I also remembered my first outing in the garden upon arrival. We came from a flat in the city on the other side of the country, and moving to a house with a large garden was a massive adventure. My parents had hesitated to purchase the house. Could they afford it? What about the massive garden? Their largest botanical project was hanging some plants from our balcony. My father's new boss had encouraged them to make the jump. It was a solid standalone house built by a builder, prewar. We would be the second family living in the house. He said it would be a very good investment. He was right. Purchasing that house was something they never regretted. To tackle the challenging large garden and substantial mortgage, half of the plot was sold immediately. Another house would eventually be built next to our property. Having jumped out of the removal van, I stretched my legs and wandered into the garden. It was a warm day. The soil was dry. I had never experienced something like that: the vast space, so much nature. My attention was drawn everywhere. My mother and sister followed the movers into the house. I loved to be by myself for a bit and explore. The house had been empty for a few months, and the garden was a bit wild. I wandered around and looked inside a flower and saw a giant spider. (I was a city boy, remember?) My heart nearly stopped, and I ran to safety inside the house. Later that day, my one-and-a-half-year-old sister decided to drink some warm water mixed with detergent to clean floors from a bucket that stood unattended. There was excitement all around; that made for two near-death experiences in one day! We had arrived in the village. I was a hyperactive little city boy. For months my parents could hear me yelling from long distances, playing with my new friends. Eventually I calmed down and became a village boy myself.

Today I entered the house from the back, as per normal. My father was no longer there to make coffee. It felt very strange. I received a warm embrace from my sister. She and my brother-in-law had already made good progress. Several things were being sorted. Books were organized in piles on the ground of the living room. I asked my sister whether she had come across a small red book, which I had given to my mother when she was terminally ill in 1993. It contained prayers and poems by Toon Hermans, a beloved conferencier. We had a tearful moment when we found it. I opened it. On the first page was a handwritten note from me to my mother, expressing my love and wishing her all the best in her battle. I turned the page over. On the next page, my mother had written a note to my father. The gist of it was that although they would soon be separated, they would still be near to one another in spirit, connected. Then, on the next page, I found a final note from my mother to me, expressing her hope that it would take many years for me to receive this book back, and thanking me for the son I had been. Tears had been there when I first read her words many years ago, following her death. And those tears were back again, now nearly three decades later. I was holding something very special.

My sister and I surveyed various cupboards. My father had kept some of my mother's special clothing items in the wardrobe upstairs. It was interesting to consider that several furniture items in the house had been part of the household for as long as my parents were married: my father's desk, a small cupboard with bookshelves. I can still remember playing around these bits of furniture when we were small. That they remained here said something about my parents—how careful they were with their belongings, and the simplicity of them. These items did their jobs. Why change them? It felt a bit strange to see them labeled to be shipped out. We simply could not take it all. We hoped all these special items would find a good home.

We were also surprised by some shopping items my father had gathered over the years. He had clearly been tempted by recurring "good offers," leading to supplies that would last various lifetimes. Ah well. I wonder whether our children have similar experiences when we pass away.

My sister and I divided some items that were on my father's desk— some of his pens and a simple black plastic container—for both of us to have items on our desks to remember him. They were simple items with profound memories. My father's desk, his pens, his papers, they all had been important to him. How many hours had he spent behind this desk? We could almost see him sitting there.

We had some lunch in the kitchen. In the past, we had all our family meals in the kitchen, except on Christmas, when we would have our meal in the living room. We loved our kitchen. It was the warmest place in the house. Looking at the small white table, I was amazed the four of us always had our meals at it. It looked so small now. It certainly was cozy— "*gezellig*," in Dutch. I remember having cups of tea and biscuits here after school. I also remember a funny incident with my sister. She must have been six, seven, or eight, and I four yours older. It was a Saturday evening. We always had a Saturday night special. There was no warm meal. We had bread, soup, and some form of snack—"*loempia*" (an Indonesian fried delicacy) or a "*kroket*" (a Dutch fried specialty) or some form of sausage. My sister was wearing a brand-new crème-colored turtleneck blouse and was squeezing a tube of ketchup or mustard, aimed toward herself. It did not quite go as expected, and a large blob ended up on her new prized possession. Live and learn. I laughed (schadenfreude kicks in at an early age for sinful humanity, I am afraid), and she looked at me and became very angry, blaming me for the accident! It was a vicious flare-up. What had I, Mr. Innocent, done? Well, I was the last person who handled the tube, and obviously my greasy fingers had caused this unfortunate event, which would never had happened if I had not been around. We all had a good laugh after the initial burst of emotion had passed.

Back to the present. My father had instructed us to give gifts to various people who had looked after him. One of our tasks for this day was to visit a number of these people, thank them for their care, and hand them their gifts. My sister took care of a number of the carers during the days she was in the house. I would visit two sets of people later in the afternoon. One family we would visit together—the couple across the road.

Coffee across the Road

We went across the road straight after lunch. Now a spacious corner house, we remembered it as the butcher's shop. You might remember my Saturday-morning episode. When we had arrived in the village, an old butcher and his wife were running the shop. A funny thing would happen when a few raucous teenage boys from the secondary school nearby would cycle by and shout, "Hey butcher, do you still have those pork trotters?" He would then come trotting out of the shop with his bloody apron on, sticking a large knife in the air, running after them. It was much fun. The butcher later sold the business to his apprentice, who stayed in the shop for several decades. Although they now lived elsewhere, the new butcher had driven my father to some hospital appointments. He and his wife also attended my father's funeral. One of my tasks as a boy had been to do some of the shopping, such as the weekly shopping at a nearby supermarket and the early Saturday-morning shopping at the bakery. I also would do the midweek shopping at the butcher's as needed, quite often for recurring items. One year, at the midsummer fair, the butcher had a challenge. If you were able to cut off one hundred grams of a certain sausage, within a five-gram margin of error, you could take the sausage with you for free; otherwise, you had to pay for it. Having seen him perform this particular act on so many occasions, it almost felt like stealing candy from a baby. He was not entirely happy when he handed me the knife, as he knew what would happen next. Yes, the sausage was mine! No, I was not allowed to have another go.

I have some other memories involving this house. When I was young, during one of the renovations in our place, I had been ill and was allowed to stay in a bed above the butcher's shop. I had been quite ill and would view the activity in our house and on the street from the bed. I would return home each evening when the builders had left. Later my place upstairs over the shop was taken by a German shepherd called Santos, who would stick his dark snout under the white curtains, peering outside, resembling a Spanish bride. At least that is what we imagined a Spanish bride to look like. Yes, I am sorry, people of Spain.

The couple now living in that house had done weekly shopping for my father and had kept an eye on him along with other neighbors. They welcomed us, and after a brief tour downstairs, we sat down for coffee. We handed them the envelope. They opened it but did not want to receive it. We replied that we were under the strict instructions of my father. They smiled and did some head shaking. They shared some stories about my father. They remembered how much he had enjoyed a particular birthday party at their place. They also commiserated on how his health and walking had deteriorated over the years and how fast he had gone downhill in the last few weeks. We thanked them for all they did for my father. "No, no thanks needed," they replied. "It was what you did …"

Home for Sale

We had to return to the house. Much needed to be done in the afternoon. We sat down for a moment to gather our thoughts and strategize on what would be next. The doorbell rang. We welcomed the real-estate agent. He was very tall, wearing a suit and glasses. He looked neat, and he had local roots. We established that his parents probably had been clients on my newspaper round forty years prior. He was a partner in a real-estate agency together with the son of a primary school teacher of my sister. Everyone connected. His company was chosen by my father. We were happy to go along with his choice. He knew the house by sight and had passed it on many occasions, wondering why the side shutters were always closed. That would be something to change for the viewings. We mentioned that the house was built in 1930 and we had been the second family living in it. Our stint of fifty-two years had been respectable. We had an initial chat, and then we went through the house from top to bottom. We then walked through the garden and showed the garage. Every corner and cranny was looked into. The realtor was very knowledgeable about construction matters and about the market—a great combination. He was careful to manage our expectations. Yes, it was a beautiful house, but the market had cooled somewhat because of to the war in Ukraine and the energy prices. Mortgages were also more difficult to obtain as a result. The house was well maintained and had double glazing, but no major work had happened since the seventies, when my parents undertook two major renovations. Lots of work likely needed to be done. We nodded. Old houses like this, objects of hot desire a few years prior, were less popular now. However, he was sure the house would sell well with the right pricing and marketing. He carefully explained the whole process.

He and my sister, a notary, got on like a house on fire when it came to the administrative nitty gritty. This was lovely to watch from the sidelines. We were in good hands. We reached agreement on commission and an action plan. We had some serious work to do to get the house ready. It needed to be cleared in two phases. Phase one would involve decluttering to take photos for the website and for the viewings that were to follow. Phase two of the clearing would need to happen just before the sale would be finalized. He then left. We were very content with what we had discussed, but I had an uneasy niggle in the back of my mind that all this was really happening. This house we knew so well, our family home, which had so many stories and memories attached to it, would be gone. However, this was meant to be. It was all right. Life moved on, but still.

My sister and I discussed the work that would ensue over the coming days and weeks. I filled the car and made my way to the two sets of people who needed to be seen and thanked. They had been involved in helping my father over many years. I visited the first friend. She now lived a few streets away. Her family used to live farther down our street. Her youngest sister had been a friend of my sister, and she herself had worked in the same hospital as my mother. Her parents, also in their mideighties, remained good friends of my father even after their move to another part of the village. I had texted her earlier, and yes, I could pop by for a cup of tea.

I parked the car around the corner so it would be easy to drive on to my last visit. I rang the doorbell. She was glad to see me. I received a warm welcome. How was Janine? How were the children? Yes, she was doing well. We spoke a bit about the funeral and about all the things that had happened since, and all that still needed to happen. It was all moving very quickly. She missed him. For years she would help my father with getting bank transfers posted (my father was among some of the last people in the Netherlands not using a computer) or doing some local shopping. Most important for my father were her visits, their friendship, and the company they shared while having a cup of tea or a glass of port. We were chatting in her kitchen. She prepared some tea for us. Hers was a lovely light house. She had lived here with her husband, who had died of a form of blood cancer far too early in his life. She never remarried. She still missed him. Missing a much-loved soul partner was a painful experience she shared with my father. They had a shared grief.

We moved to the living room and sat down. I presented her with the envelope containing the card and gift. She was genuinely surprised. It was too much, she said. She could not accept it. I assured her, just as with the other couple, that I was heeding my father's instructions. She stood and gave me an embrace. She was a dear friend. We chatted a bit more over tea and she saw me out. We chatted a bit more by the car. We would stay in touch. I closed the car window. We waved. The lane was dark as I passed the large, stately trees. I was now close to the edge of the forest. We always came this way for our family walks on Sunday afternoons.

The final visit of the day was to some friends living in the forest. The mother of the woman who lived there with her husband had been a colleague of my father. I had known the family for decades. I entered their long drive from the main road. The curved path was edged by birch trees and heather. I had been to this house on so many occasions. I parked in the clearing and walked to the front door. I could hear a big dog making his way to the door. The door opened. The dog was massive but fortunately was firmly held. Was it a dog or a pony? "Do not worry. He is very friendly," the owner assured me. Great!

The three of us were sitting in their living room, staring into the clearing around the house, which was completely covered in leaves. Gathering the leaves would require several days. Work would start tomorrow. We drank our coffee. We talked a bit about the funeral, the final months of my father. They had also helped my father over many years: a hot meal on a Tuesday, help with Friday shopping in the market, the occasional visit to a hospital or eye specialist in a town not nearby. This living room came with happy memories too. My father's colleague had been a good pianist. On a number of occasions, I had played together with her, she on the piano and I on the violin. It was good family fun. How often we had come for a cup of tea, only to leave so much later in the evening after drinks and nibbles. I can still see my mother cycling down the hill with a certain swagger. These are precious memories. They also received the envelope with protestations.

I reported to them on the events of that day: the visit of the realtor, the clearing my sister and I had managed to do. Had I found the album with photos of this woman's mother's farewell party at her place of work? She had lent it to my father during his illness to help him remember times past and old colleagues. She described the album to me. I did not remember having seen it, but I promised I would keep my eyes open the next time I was in the house. It was now getting dark. I needed to get back home. We said farewell. We would stay in touch. I made my way to the highway, filling up before making my way back home. It had been a full and special day.

The next day, I made an important phone call. We were given a contact by the church to help us clear the house. I made an appointment by phone. Yes, the man on the line knew my father. Everyone knew my father. Actually, this man's son had been my father's gardener for several years. The son was indeed known to us. We made an appointment. He would visit the next time I was in the village. That day would come soon.

Day with My Family

This morning we arrived from quite a different direction. We had spent some days in our apartment at the coast during a school break. Midmorning we made our way to my father's home. We would do some more sorting. We would take a few important things with us, and we would meet with several people during the day.

I opened the front door—a first. I don't think I had ever entered the house this way. The house felt cold. My first move was to the thermostat to turn the heating up. The house was again filled with chatter, activity, and life. The front door stayed open a bit long. I could imagine my father's disapproval: "The heating is on!" I smiled. "Yes, Dad, I will take care of it."

One of my main objectives was to locate my parents' wedding Bible. I found it rather quickly. My sister had already separated a number of family Bibles and church books. Their wedding Bible, it was so precious to hold. This was the Bible we would read after dinner. I opened it. The opening page showed Romans 8:32 in the handwriting (fountain pen) of the vicar who had married my parents, now nearly sixty years ago. At the back of the Bible were two orders of service from their wedding. I can almost imagine these two copies being held by my parents in the service and lovingly put in the Bible afterward. There was also a copy of the marriage form, which had been read out in the service and used for marriage preparation. "This is what Christian marriage is about …" We also found a newspaper clipping of my maternal grandfather. As a young man, on a cold night off the coast of France, he had dived into the cold sea to save a friend. The news clipping showed a photo of a tall young man, his much smaller parents behind him. He was standing tall to receive a medal from a vice admiral in recognition of his courageous deed. We were stunned at seeing that photo. How much our teenage son resembled him. It never crossed my mind, but here it was before us. After his death, his medals, which he had received for numerous acts of valor during his life, saving people from the sea, were donated to the local museum. Memories of him flashed before my eyes: my sleepovers with him and my grandmother, my holidays with them on their small motor cruiser, the fishing, the rowing, the things he taught me, our visits to the harbor and the lifeboat he had skippered. I can still see this tall silver-haired man in a dark blue suit, coat, and hat, smoking a hand-rolled cigarette, sitting on the bench outside my school, picking me up for lunch.

We made various labels and notes to make it easy for people to do the first phase of clearing the house. Some serious decluttering was happening. Again we loaded in the car various things that we wanted to preserve— things to remind us of my father and mother. It was challenging to progress. Almost every item, cupboard, or corner I came across had a story. Our two youngest had much fun exploring the house. I searched for my kids. They were upstairs. I told them some more stories about our bedrooms. For example, how my late reading was detected by our cleaning lady as she cycled by one late evening. We also went to my parents' bedroom. This was the room where my mother had died, and I remembered seeing her body one stormy Saturday evening. I did not share this memory. We looked at my mother's dressing table—another piece of furniture from the sixties. It was a low brown table with large foldable mirrors mounted on top. Here we found my mother's stethoscope, which she had used as a nurse. This was an excellent memento for my eldest daughter, who was now in her fifth year of medicine. She was also named after my mother, whom sadly she had never known. When we returned home, she was very pleased with it. I had just a few items to remind me of my mother, some received after she died; these included some jewelry, the small red book with her precious personal message, a few photos, and this stethoscope, plus many, many precious memories.

The Iraqi couple from a few houses away rang the doorbell. I knew from my sister they were going to drop by to pick up a few things and we needed to discuss when they would pick up one of their bikes stored in the garage. We laughed as they came into the front door, because as with so many others, they had never used that door. Everyone came in around the back. I knew how they felt. We chatted about the funeral as we walked through the house. My son helped them carry some of the items my father wanted them to have. Bits of furniture and other things that would come in handy. They invited us for a meal, which was very generous. Sadly, it was not possible for us to make it on that occasion, but I promised we would stop by on a next visit. It struck me what a beautiful blend of people had gathered around my father over the years: friends old and new; Christians from various countries and denominations, and various non-Christians; neighbors, both old and younger. It was a diverse and rich human family. They were all people with their own challenges but sharing life and looking after each other in an expression of loving and caring humanity. It was a foretaste of heaven. We live in hope!

At the same time, another family friend stopped by. She was one of the people I had visited with an envelope the previous week. She came to thank us again and to wish us well with the amount of work that still needed to be done. She also brought some delicacies from the local patisserie.

As we were coming to the end of our clearing session for the day, a man stopped by. He was the one who would organize a team to clear the house. We had briefly spoken on the phone the previous week. His organization was linked with the church. We would pay a very reasonable sum to cover all travel expenses. He explained almost apologetically that fuel prices had risen substantially. Any proceeds from the sale of furniture and other items would go to the church. This was a very practical service to the community and to the church. I explained that the house needed to be cleared in two stages. The first stage was for the house to be decluttered to make it ready for photos and viewings. The final clearing would take place before the house would be sold. He nodded. That was a sensible way to do it. He and the team did this regularly. I was glad it happened like this. It gave us a bit more time to sort through things and decide. It was all going very quickly anyway.

We walked through the house and discussed what needed to stay and what needed to go in this first stage. Clarity was all-important, so I promised that we would clearly mark everything in comprehensive piles. I took him with me to meet the couple across the road, who would provide him with the key. We rang the bell. The door opened. Yes, they knew each other from the market. Everyone knew each other. I should have known by now. After a friendly brief exchange, we were all done. We walked back across the road. We shook hands. He unlocked his bike and was off. I went back inside to finish my sorting and labeling job for today. As I was going through the various items, so many stories bubbled to the surface. However, I needed to focus. A job needed to be done. I had various discussions with Janine on what would be handy to take now and what was better left for my next visit. We decided to use some of the built-in wardrobes as storage to keep things simple for the clearing team. We were making good progress. When the team had passed through, we could envisage the house as being ready for the photographer. My goodness, how much stuff does one gather in a lifetime? I wondered whether we would do better in the decluttering department when our time came. We packed up, turned the thermostat down, and closed the house. Off we went, again.

A few nights later, I woke in the middle of the night out of a dream where I had marked a precious item (a toy box made by my grandfather) to be taken away. I was quite relieved to find the box in place on my next visit to the house.

Paul Vrolijk

One Month Later

As mentioned previously, one of my daughters had not been able to attend the funeral. This had been traumatic for her and had been sad for us. We now had a chance to take her with us to visit my father's home and his grave. The weather on the road was similar as on that special day two months before when I was on my way to my father in the hospital to discuss treatment options with his doctors. Today was exactly one month after my father's funeral. So much had happened in these past few weeks. It was almost a blur.

The opening of and entering the house through the front door, the cold and empty hallway, the move to the thermostat to turn the heating up, an empty house, the cold—this was all becoming familiar now. There were some leaves in the hallway from the first removal phase. We turned the central heating up and went to the kitchen to see whether we could make some coffee. We had some lunch and started to look at various rooms to decide what could be done today.

We went through the house. The removal team had done a fantastic job. The cellar and loft were completely empty now. I vacuumed the loft. Though it was now very empty, I remembered this had been a place with mystique. In the early years, a twin bed had been here. My grandparents would sleep here when they stayed with us for a few days. When we were small, my sister and I would creep up the creaky set of narrow stairs to snuggle up with my grandparents as they were just waking up. The loft was also the place where things we did not use that often were stored: skates; Christmas gear, such as the green plastic stand in which the tree would be placed, and bags of boxes of silver balls and tinsel; stuff acquired by my parents early in their marriage. There had been an annual feast of recognition of older and newer treasures. This was also the place where camping equipment was stored in two large wooden crates. How did one camp with those large crates anyway? I just did not remember how we had travelled with all this gear, not having a car. That is something I forgot to ask my father. Not that I remembered us ever using the "bungalow" tent again after a fateful wet summer when I was three years old and we were washed away in the middle of the night. Anyway, it was stored well in the loft. And then, a few decades later, the disintegrated tent was thrown away. My parents clearly were not great campers. Life itself was adventure enough. The wooden crates, however, stayed.

On my birthday during a very hot summer, the stair mechanism of the creaky stairs leading to the loft had broken down after decades of service. The rope holding the counterweight had completely disintegrated. Eventually a new, lighter modern set of foldable stairs was installed.

I continued the vacuum cleaning on the lower floors. It was starting to look like a house ready for viewings.

When we were finished in the house, we closed up and made our way to the cemetery. We parked next to the church. The last signs of the morning market were being removed. The three of us took the same route through the cemetery as on the day of the funeral. The familiar names and the familiar stones were there once again. I shared some of the stories. We arrived at the grave. Various ornate flower pieces had been left on the grave after the funeral. Something amazing had happened. It was almost as if nature had absorbed the handcrafted flower arrangements and transformed them back into itself. It was quite stunning. I kept looking at it, not quite believing what had happened. I took some photos. The stone would be returned after my father's name and some text had been added. Normally these things take a few months, and I was thinking of returning in the spring, when everything would have been taken care of. Was I anticipating complete closure? I wasn't so sure. It was a difficult moment for my daughter. A grandfather she had loved dearly was gone. We spent a moment standing next to the grave on the wet grass. His absence was definite.

We walked back from the grave on another beautiful autumn day. This gave me the chance to take a closer look at the giant acacia at the back of church. My father's home run was marked by a crescendo of acacias. We turned around the corner from the church. One market stand was left from the Friday-morning market on the parking area adjacent to the church. "Beemster kaas. Kaas boer Annie" (the cheese man and his wife). This was clearly a family venture. The cheese couple. We recognized the name from the wrappers we had seen over the years. We introduced ourselves. The husband-and-wife team stopped their work and smiled. Yes, they had known my father. They were sorry for our loss. They had heard. We received their condolences. I remembered the husband from a shopping trip to the market several decades ago. He had the same lean face, just older. My father had been a client for forty-six years. The link went even further back, as the cheese man's father had been a client of my father for the Internal Revenue Service. The couple had fond memories of my father.

Cars were occasionally trying to make their way around a cheese advertisement banner pinned to the pavement. The couple were completely unfazed by the encroaching traffic that was slowly trying to reclaim the parking areas taken over by the market. The wife also remembered my mother and told me I reminded her of her. They then shared some memories of my father. They stated that, over the years, he had bought cheese that needed to be wrapped for his son in the UK. Yes, that was me. And for his son in France. Yes, that was me. We remembered my father visiting us in our apartment on the coast. I would pick him up from a nearby station and, having arrived, he would sit down and open his shopping bag of goodies. It was a ritual. Grandchildren would be standing around in glad expectation. One standard item was the vacuum-packed cheese. This was a tradition for many, many years. The cheese couple then remarked on how poor my father's walking had been for the past few years and said that on occasion he would take a seat in their stand if there was a long line. They also recalled how my father would open his wallet and how particular he would be when he ordered everything in just the right way. I could see my father standing there, slightly bent, peering into his wallet and being fastidious in ordering his notes and his bits, a checkered cloth cap covering his thinning hair. How precious, these through-and-through normal exchanges knitting the human family together over time. Vast volumes of cheese had been exchanged bit by bit in exchange for well-organized money.

We warmly left one another. My daughter disappeared to buy a coffee for the road. We got back into the car and slowly made our way out of the village center, the stately, majestic trees bidding us farewell in the glorious autumn sun. What a remarkable series of visits to this village that was so precious to me. I felt held and comforted every step of the way.

Emails and calls

Following an advertisement in the local village newspaper, more reactions came in. Some were from people who knew my father from various shops;

others were from people who knew him from the neighborhood. Two messages were extra special. One message came from my best friend in primary school. He and his family lived two houses down. We arrived in the village during the summer, and in August we both went to the first class in primary school (Dutch Reformed), two streets away. For six years, we did everything together. We played a lot of soccer on the Roman Catholic school playground farther down our street. Two memories of our time stick out to me. One is the picking of blackberries next to the nearby railroad. We collected buckets full of them for juice. It was quite something to be in the midst of thorny bushes on a steep bank, with the occasional yellow train passing by within meters of us. The other adventure had to do with fruit from the earth as well—potatoes. One damp Saturday morning in autumn, I joined his family to harvest potatoes in a village a few kilometers away—something I had never witnessed or done as a true city boy. In their car, we drove to the village. A local farmer offered the option to people to harvest their own potatoes. What an adventure! I was on my knees in my old clothes in the wet soil as we dug the potatoes with our hands. After a few hours, the whole back of their car was filled with self-harvested potatoes. My parents got part of the treasure as well. Never was making my hands dirty such a pleasure. My friend had gone to a different school after primary. We would see each other occasionally. His parents eventually moved to a different street. We would see each other in church. Years later I visited him in the shop down the street. It was great to receive his message and his condolences. He had stopped with the shop many years prior and was employed elsewhere, married with three grown daughters, still living in the village.

One of the people who contacted us was our old history teacher from secondary school. He and my father had met regularly in the village. My father had reported on my progress through life, and I had received his greetings over the years through my father. I loved history; it was possibly my favorite subject. I never considered studying it because of my youthful desire for power and prosperity. If one wanted to earn money, one did not study history or literature. Knowing what I now know, I perhaps wish I had chosen differently, but that is massive hindsight. Actually, I am totally content with the path I have taken. This teacher and I reconnected on WhatsApp. I certainly recognized him, although we had not seen each other for nearly forty years. Yes, it was very much him. It was great to be connected like this, though it was sobering to hear some of the things he lived and lives through. It was quite something to talk after so many years. We both remembered my father with gratitude.

Advertised. Shown. Sold.

We received a draft of the brochure for the house. The photographer had come around on a nice, clear day. The house looked great. On a Monday, the house was listed on the website. A number of people showed interest, and a number of viewings were booked on Friday and the following Monday. Things happened quickly. The first set of buyers were very serious—a young family, we were told. An offer was made just below the asking price. A counteroffer was made the same day. An agreement was reached the next day. Viewings for the Monday were cancelled. Things were moving fast indeed. The buyers wanted to move quickly, as their house had sold and they needed to move out in a few weeks.

The moment an agreement was reached, there was a part of me that felt profound sadness. Having nearly received the asking price was nice, but did it really matter compared with everything we had experienced in our home: belonging, living, blessed and hallowed normality? It had always been there for us. Seeing the house that had been such a place of love, welcoming, and familiarity disappear from our lives would be hard, but it had to happen. It would have been impossible to keep the house. That would have been silly. A family needed to live there. The neighborhood needed to be blessed with new blood, new life, laughter and play, people who would become part of a community. But there was an inner sense of loss. This is life: being blessed and letting go, giving and releasing for flourishing.

In this period, we also received a few messages from people who had seen the photos on the real-estate website and who were interested in particular items. We found out that a number of these so-called interested individuals were antiques buyers. That was all fine, of course. Having reached agreement with the church related clearing team, we decided not to engage with such offers so as to keep things simple.

Last Visit to the House

Earlier journeys had taken place in glorious sunshine. Today was very different. There was frost and thick fog for most of that day. With my daughter from England, I drove that now so familiar stretch. How many times had I done this over the past few months? I could look it up, but the visits blended into one another. The exchange would take place in five days. We needed to do a few more things. This was our last chance to visit the house, to see and remember it how it was, though we might be back, who knows when, to say hello to the new owners and see how another chapter has started.

We arrived at the house. I parked in front, halfway on the drive and the pavement, to aid the packing we needed to do. I entered the house. It was colder now than on the last visit. I turned the thermostat up. I walked through the house. We discussed what needed to be done and when we wanted to be heading back. A man rang the doorbell. I opened the door. A tall man asked whether that was my car on the drive. I thought I was blocking his way, but no, that was not the problem. As he cycled by, he noticed that one of my tires was very low. Did I know? How attentive and kind. I thanked him! He walked back to his bike and was off. We waved. This morning the car diagnostics had indicated there was a problem with another tire; this one I had not noticed. I could see this could have become a problem in the frosty conditions. I was grateful and amazed. This would not have happened in the city. Minding one's own business would be the higher priority for most there.

Going through a large cupboard with coffee cups and glasses, I came across a thick brown photo album. I opened it and immediately knew this was the missing album of my father's colleague. I called the daughter, and she was delighted. She told me she would stop by later in the morning to pick it up. I was so glad this was found. These photos were unique, and I am sure they would have been thrown out in the final clearing.

I went back into the house, where I had some more sorting and packing to do. *What to take and what to leave? What are my reasons for taking things?* I made a brief visit to the garage. I wanted to bring a few garden tools back as well, and the low step-in bike. I quickly visited the couple across the road to say farewell and to inform them about the team that would come on Thursday. Yes, they had heard already. They would be here. We smiled and said good-bye.

Our friend stopped by to pick up the album. She was so pleased we had found it. This was another loose end taken care of. Every detail was falling into place. We embraced in a firm hug. Yes, we would stay in touch.

The Iraqi couple from two houses down came to take their bike from the garage, and we asked them whether they were interested in some items, including a washing machine and dining table. They had blessed my father with soup, meals and friendship over many years. They had borrowed garden chairs and tables for family events and had been very good to my father. They were brothers and sisters in Christ. They helped me move a special item—the toy box my grandfather had made for me half a century ago—from upstairs into the car. The "what his eyes saw …" grandfather. You know. On a previous visit, we had promised the Iraqi couple that we would visit them for a coffee or a meal on our next visit. We promised now that we would visit them when we were finished for the day. They are such warm and generous people. They left, and we went back into the house to sort through some more photos. The car was quite full now. After one last inspection, we walked around the corner to visit the Iraqi couple and had a wonderful time with them, hearing their story and of the current state of their church, which is now scattered around the globe, having been forced out of their home nation by violence. When we left, we were given some warm spring rolls. Back in the house, I ate two before getting ready to leave. They were delicious.

I walked through the house one last time, feeling grateful for the immense blessings that were bestowed on me in this place. In the dead normality, it felt like a very blessed and light moment. It was hallowed emptiness. I felt as if it had gone from home to shell. I needed to leave. We needed to be on the road again. I could not stay.

I closed the door. I removed the keys from the worn leather pouch—another small reminder of my father. How many times had he held it? How many times had he checked the keys were really in there? I would carry it with me. I pushed the two keys through the letterbox and heard them clatter on the tiles in the hallway. A chapter closed. I turned away. We entered the stuffed car and drove off in the frosty fog, soon making a quick visit to the gas station to pump the tires. All was well; there was no leak, it seems. We were ready for our return. It would be another long journey. There was much to sort through, especially in my mind and in my heart. The loss of not returning to that place of blessing has not yet caught up with me. I am still moving too fast. Or is it fleeing not to be feeling?

Sunday Afternoon

I was writing a few words about my last visit. A text came in from my sister. She and my brother-in-law had finished the last bits. They had met with the buyers. She had now also given her keys to the neighbors across the street. Thursday morning the team would come in to clear the last bits of furniture, clothing, crockery, and so forth. In early afternoon, the real estate agents and buyers would inspect the house before heading to the notary for the exchange. We were delighted a young family would move in and transform the place. We prayed that the house would be a place of blessing, as it had been for us.

***

I am typing my tentative words to hold what I cannot hold. I still try. I am listening to Eamonn Dougan: "Keep me as the apple of your eye … hide me under the shadow of your wing." So kept. So precious. Held. Now the tears are coming as I see my elderly father—bent, walking with difficulty—having known his gentle love, his care, and his kind and responsible looking after us and so many others. Simple, yet profound. Boring, yet hallowed. Beyond valuation. Treasure of my heart.

Final Days

The final days of owning the house were taken up by checking plenty of contract details for the notary and the final arrangements for getting the last things out of the house. My sister had met with the new owners, and the little girl was looking forward to feeding the birds. I needed to instruct the cleaning team, "Yes, the birdhouse needs to stay." I am glad I did. It would have been taken. Devil and details …

Thursday Evening

A few hours prior to writing this, I received the message that the sale of my father's house was completed without any complications. The team managed to clear everything in time in the morning. Heroes! I called the team to thank them. The real estate agent came for a final inspection. Afterward the buyers had made their way to the notary for the final exchange. My sister and I did not manage to attend, but all was taken care of. The house was no longer in the family. This was a very strange feeling. A young family would sleep in the house tomorrow night. A new chapter would be started.

I now sit at the dining table, staring into the garden. It is a dark winter's evening. I can see the dark evening sky over the rooftops of the houses at the back of our house. Frost on the lawn. A candle is lit. Sacred music is playing. I feel a mix of sadness and great bliss. The past three months have been extraordinary, from the day of those discussions with my father in the hospital, to hospice, to graveside, to clearing a family home. This month comes with an extra milestone. In three days, it will be sixty years ago when my parents got married. One photo of their wedding day is etched on my mind's eye. They are walking arm in arm, my mother in white, my father in a dark dinner jacket with tails and a top hat. They look so young. Both are smiling. I can almost see them sitting next to each other in church, holding their wedding service liturgies and receiving their wedding Bible. This brings to mind Romans 8. Soon their gravestone, bearing the same scripture reference, will be placed on their grave. More closure is on the way.

Afterword

Closure?

COMING TO THE END OF WRITING ABOUT THE SOBERING AND YET glorious events surrounding my father's death feels strange. It has been four months now since I last visited my father at home. As I said, it all happened fairly quickly: hospital, hospice, death, funeral, and clearing and selling the house. On reflection I am amazed how smoothly everything went. Other parts of my life know plenty of challenge, but the closing part of my father's life—the conversations, the discussions, the visits, our farewell in stages, the arrangements—it all just flowed. I see tremendous blessing in that provision. I am filled with gratitude. Our days are in your hand, O Lord. On another level, all this still has not sunk in yet. On numerous occasions, the thought has crossed my mind to call my father, just to catch up and have a chat. Then, of course, there comes the realization that a simple call is not possible anymore. My father's house sold rapidly. The stone on the grave of my mother and father has now been adjusted and will be replaced again soon. I am still sorting through memories. Writing has been a tremendous help for that and, more importantly, has allowed me to savor the sweet memory of my father. In so many ways, we were so different, yet I am his son who was loved and cared for by him. Eighty-five years he lived, and he cared not just for me, but for many. He did what he could, at his pace and in his way. He will remain a treasure in my heart and an inspiration. If nobody reads these words, this process will still have fulfilled its purpose. However, I *do* hope that people will read these words to bring about healing, comfort, wholeness, and encouragement. The last phase of a loved one's life can be very precious.

I have also had more time now to reflect on the various things my father prepared. What are the things that have inspired me? What things will I adapt and try to do in my own way when the time comes? So many of the things my father did, prepared, arranged, and asked for flowed from the caring, kind, humble, uncomplicated, generous person he was. He was organized, but not willfully controlling. He saved a princely sum over many, many years for all the grandchildren. They were given equal, generous parts. He prepared gifts for all the people who looked after him. He expressed desire regarding hope being given in his funeral service, not a reigning beyond the grave. He had an organized, caring mind, not a controlling hand. And he had an open, generous heart for a final warm farewell. Delayed love gift.

Could he have decluttered a bit more? Probably. Does it matter? It does not. I am so grateful for the connections with bits from my upbringing—not as a dwelling on nostalgia, but as a reminder for gratitude, a moving toward the rest of my life, more living from the perspective of the end, and a longing for more discerned living—having a better sense to see the difference between wheat and chaff, between noise and heavenly tones. At least that is my intention. When I fail, and I will, I will endeavor to do so with self-compassion. He would not mind.

As mentioned, a lot has happened in these last four months. The house has been emptied and sold. There are still some boxes of special books, items, and belongings to sort through. "How am I doing?" I ask myself. I remember that, following my mother's funeral, a real wave of grief hit me six weeks later. I still remember it vividly. Janine and I were doing the dishes on a Saturday night when grief suddenly washed over me. Will this time be different?

I also realize that a tremendous amount of administration has taken place (thanks to my sister). Are there mental, emotional, or spiritual loose ends I am not aware of? What is lurking below the surface of consciousness that is about to break cover? I still feel tremendous gratitude for my father's life and for how we have done over the past few weeks together as a family. So much good has happened. I remain full of admiration for the various things my father prepared over the years. His generosity and care continue to touch me.

How will things unfold in our family now that the parental home is no longer there? I am hopeful. I am thinking of my relationship with my sister. Though our lives and directions are different, there is much that binds us together. And the refining experience of travelling together in this season of transition has welded us together. The closing words of my father are not weighing us down but are encouraging us to seek the higher road, to seek love always. Also with the wider family, bonds remain healthy. A date for next year's barbecue has already been set for July, when we would celebrate my father's birthday. It is lovely that this will happen.

Where was God? Ignatius of Loyola encourages us to find God in all things. I love that, and I have been trying to live that maxim for many years now. Looking back over the last few months, I can discern God's hand and God's loving and guiding presence in so many ways, including God's presence in glorious nature, which reminds us of the Giver of Life, who is always there, always present, and never far away; the so-called coincidences; the amazing provisions; the people who came on our path; the kindness we experienced in so many ways; the many people who helped and comforted us; and the gentle ways challenges were met and overcome. Yes, we had to do our bit, but God was there. Christ was all in all. God was in all things. He was in the utterly practical and pedestrian details of end-of-life care and funerals, as well as the grand and lofty realities of the spiritual realms. It was all held by the One. How wonderful it is to know we are part of that. We are all invited to come and have our eyes opened to that greater reality.

Yes, my grandparents were right: "For none of us lives to himself, and none of us dies to himself. For if we live, we live to the Lord, and if we die, we die to the Lord. So then, whether we live or whether we die, we are the Lord's. For to this end Christ died and lived again, that he might be Lord both of the dead and of the living" (Romans 14:7–9). We do not live for ourselves. And we do not die for ourselves. My father lived those words so well.

And yes, our present-day suffering is nothing compared to the glory that is to be revealed. My father's suffering was challenging for him, but it enabled us to spend time together, to focus on what truly mattered, and to say our farewells properly. Also, a few years ago we moved somewhat closer to him, which enabled us to see him more often than before. That was a blessing as well. Things had been brought to a close beautifully.

Yes, my parents were right in starting their married life with these hallowed words, which came back time and time again: "What, then, shall we say in response to these things? If God is for us, who can be against us? He who did not spare his own Son, but gave him up for us all—how will he not also, along with him, graciously give us all things?" (Romans 8:31–32).

Will He not give us all things? He has.

Nothing can separate us from the Love of God in Christ Jesus, our Lord.

Bless you as you go. The Lord be with you.

He will be.

Appendix A

Readings

"Do not let your hearts be troubled. You believe in God; believe also in me. ² My Father's house has many rooms; if that were not so, would I have told you that I am going there to prepare a place for you? ³ And if I go and prepare a place for you, I will come back and take you to be with me that you also may be where I am. ⁴ You know the way to the place where I am going." ⁵ Thomas said to him, "Lord, we don't know where you are going, so how can we know the way?" ⁶ Jesus answered, "I am the way and the truth and the life. No one comes to the Father except through me. ⁷ If you really know me, you will know my Father as well. From now on, you do know him and have seen him." (John 14:1–7 NIV)

³¹ What, then, shall we say in response to these things? If God is for us, who can be against us? ³² He who did not spare his own Son, but gave him up for us all—how will he not also, along with him, graciously give us all things?³³ Who will bring any charge against those whom God has chosen? It is God who justifies. ³⁴ Who then is the one who condemns? No one. Christ Jesus who died—more than that, who was raised to life—is at the right hand of Godand is also interceding for us. ³⁵ Who shall separate us from the love of Christ? Shall trouble or hardship or persecution or famine or nakedness or danger or sword? ³⁶ As it is written:

"For your sake we face death all day long;
we are considered as sheep to be slaughtered."

37 No, in all these things we are more than conquerors through him who loved us. 38 For I am convinced that neither death nor life, neither angels nor demons, neither the present nor the future, nor any powers, 39 neither height nor depth, nor anything else in all creation, will be able to separate us from the love of God that is in Christ Jesus our Lord. (Romans 8:31–39 NIV)

New International Version

Appendix B

Hymns

For All the Saints Who from Their Labors Rest

1 For all the saints who from their labors rest,
who thee by faith before the world confessed,
thy name, O Jesus, be forever blest.
Alleluia! Alleluia!

2 Thou wast their rock, their fortress, and their might;
thou, Lord, their captain in the well-fought fight;
thou, in the darkness drear, their one true light.
Alleluia! Alleluia!

3 Oh, may thy soldiers, faithful, true, and bold
fight as the saints who nobly fought of old
and win with them the victor's crown of gold.
Alleluia! Alleluia!

4 Oh, blest communion, fellowship divine!
We feebly struggle, they in glory shine;
yet all are one in thee, for all are thine.
Alleluia! Alleluia!

5 And when the fight is fierce, the warfare long,
steals on the ear the distant triumph song,
and hearts are brave again and arms are strong.
Alleluia! Alleluia!

6 The golden evening brightens in the west;
soon, soon to faithful warriors cometh rest;
sweet is the calm of paradise the blest.
Alleluia! Alleluia!

7 But, lo! there breaks a yet more glorious day;
the saints triumphant rise in bright array;
the King of glory passes on his way.
Alleluia! Alleluia!

8 From earth's wide bounds, from ocean's farthest coast,
through gates of pearl streams in the countless host,
singing to Father, Son, and Holy Ghost,
Alleluia! Alleluia!

William Walsham How (1823-1897),
Dutch translation W. Barnard (1920-2010).
Music Ralph Vaughan Williams (1872-1958)

Er is een land van louter licht (There Is a Land of Pure Delight)

1 There is a land of pure delight,
where saints immortal reign;
infinite day excludes the night,
and pleasures banish pain.

2 There everlasting spring abides,
and never-withering flowers;
death, like a narrow sea, divides
that heavenly land from ours.

3 Sweet fields beyond the swelling flood
stand dressed in living green;
so to the Jews old Canaan stood,
while Jordan rolled between.

4 But timorous mortals start and shrink
to cross the narrow sea,
and linger shivering on the brink,
and fear to launch away.

5 O could we make our doubts remove,
those gloomy doubts that rise,
and see the Canaan that we love
with unbeclouded eyes;

6 Could we but climb where Moses stood,
and view the landscape o'er,
not Jordan's stream, nor death's cold flood,
should fright us from the shore!

From *Liedboek van de Kerken*, 1973, based on the hymn
"There Is a Land of Pure Delight" by Isaac Watts (1709).

Now Thank We All Our God

1 Now thank we all our God
with heart and hands and voices,
who wondrous things has done,
in whom his world rejoices;
who from our mothers' arms
has blessed us on our way
with countless gifts of love,
and still is ours today.

2 O may this bounteous God
through all our life be near us,
with ever joyful hearts
and blessed peace to cheer us,
to keep us in his grace,
and guide us when perplexed,
and free us from all ills
of this world in the next.

3 All praise and thanks to God
the Father now be given,
the Son and Spirit blest,
who reign in highest heaven
the one eternal God,
whom heaven and earth adore;
for thus it was, is now,
and shall be evermore.

From *Psalter Hymnal* (Gray), 1987.

Thine Be the Glory

Thine be the glory, risen, conquering Son;
endless is the victory, thou o'er death hast won;
angels in bright raiment rolled the stone away,
kept the folded grave clothes where thy body lay.

Refrain:
Thine be the glory, risen conquering Son,
Endless is the vict'ry, thou o'er death hast won.

Lo! Jesus meets us, risen from the tomb;
Lovingly he greets us, scatters fear and gloom;
let the Church with gladness, hymns of triumph sing;
for her Lord now liveth, death hath lost its sting.

Refrain:
Thine be the glory, risen conquering Son,
Endless is the vict'ry, thou o'er death hast won.

No more we doubt thee, glorious Prince of life;
life is naught without thee; aid us in our strife;
make us more than conquerors, through thy deathless love:
bring us safe through Jordan to thy home above.

Refrain:
Thine be the glory, risen conquering Son,
Endless is the vict'ry, thou o'er death hast won.

Original written in French by Edmond Budry, translated by Richard Hoyle.

Appendix **C**

Places

For those who really want to know, the village where my father lived was Bennekom, in the Netherlands. The hospital was based in Ede; the hospice, in Sassenheim. My sister lives in Leiden. Our apartment on the coast is in Katwijk. I live in Brussels.

Acknowledgments

THIS FAREWELL IS DEDICATED TO ALL WHO LOVED AND CARED FOR MY father. I hope you found yourselves on the preceding pages. I wrote this in tremendous gratitude to you!

Several people were kind and courageous enough to read rough drafts of the manuscript. Your comments have been tremendously valuable. Thank you Michael Harvey, Diane Robson, Dick Klaassen, Richard Bromley, Bob Kerssen, Danièle Réchard-Spence, Marieke de Groot, Laura Buckner, Annie Bolger, Sylvia Organ, Peronel Barnes. Thank you for your edits, comments, challenge, and encouragement, but mostly for your love at a time when I was coping with my grief. You are all wonderful friends.

I am very grateful for my sister Evelyne and her husband Paul, and for all they have done for my father over the years. This experienced has welded us closer together!

I am deeply thankful for Janine and my children, and for their steadfast love over the years and in these last few months. It has been a profound journey.

As my writing has made clear, I am deeply indebted to my parents. They have given my sister and me a wonderful start in life. We have so much to be thankful for. This book has helped me to recall all that my parents were and did. They were gifts from heaven.

My deepest gratitude, however, belongs to God: Father, Son, and Holy Spirit—the Trinity of Love. How we have been blessed in all things. In life and in death, your glory surpasses all suffering.

About the Author

PAUL VROLIJK IS A DUTCH ANGLICAN PRIEST CURRENTLY LIVING AND working in Brussels, Belgium. He is also an ICF accredited coach. Paul is the founder of Christilience.org, a nonprofit that helps people find clarity and strength for their journeys. Paul is married and has four children, two of which are still living at home. Paul is passionate about helping people reach their God-given potentials for Jesus Christ in full.

For more information, visit www.Christilience.org.

Printed in the United States
by Baker & Taylor Publisher Services